SUPPORTING
CHILD-INITIATED
LEARNING

FEATHERSTONE
AN IMPRINT OF BLOOMSBURY
LONDON   NEW DELHI   NEW YORK   SYDNEY

First edition published 2008 (reprinted 2009, 2010)
This edition published 2013 by Featherstone, an imprint of Bloomsbury Publishing Plc
50 Bedford Square,
London,
WC1B 3DP
www.bloomsbury.com

ISBN 978-1-4081-8916-0

Written by Ros Bayley, Helen Bilton, Lynn Broadbent, Jane Cole, Judith Dancer, Jan Dubiel, Sally Featherstone, Pam Lafferty, Jennie Lindon, Janet Moyles, Sue Palmer, Theodora Papatheodorou, Linda Pound, Wendy Scott

Book conceived and planned by Sally Featherstone

Typeset by Fakenham Prepress Solutions, Fakenham, Norfolk NR21 8NN
Printed by CPI Group (UK) Ltd, Croydon CR0 4YY

10 9 8 7 6 5 4 3 2 1

This book is produced using paper that is made from wood grown in managed, sustainable forests. It is natural, renewable and recyclable. The logging and manufacturing processes conform to the environmental regulations of the country of origin.

To see our full range of titles visit
www.bloomsbury.com

Contents

Preface

This book was conceived by Sally Featherstone, who invited a number of distinguished early years experts to contribute to a work on child-initiated learning. At that time there was no particular feeling about how long the book should be or what it should say, except that it should offer some definitions and views of child-initiated learning, discuss why it was important and provide guidance on stimulating and encouraging it. For that, contributors would take as much space as they felt was required in order to say what they considered to be important in relation to their chosen aspect.

All those who were approached replied enthusiastically, including those few who were unable to take part because other commitments prevented them from meeting the publication deadline.

The contributors were given a free choice to write about any aspect of child-initiated learning that particularly interested them and that they felt was specially important. Fortunately they all chose separate topics, and the work they produced falls neatly into three sections. The first defines child initiated learning and describes its characteristics; the second examines child initiated learning in key areas of the curriculum; the third looks at specific issues relating to child-initiated learning. We have assumed the reader to be a practitioner in an early years setting, although we believe that childminders, managers, advisers, indeed anyone concerned with provision for children under five, will find the book of value. The views expressed are each contributor's own.

We have used 'practitioner' throughout this book as an inclusive term to indicate any adult who cares for a child other than their own – nursery nurse or assistant, teacher, classroom assistant, childminder, day carer and so on. Pronouns, too, are a problem – and so is gender! Rather than tediously repeat 'or him' whenever we mention 'her' and 'or her' every time we mention 'him', we have referred to the child sometimes as masculine and sometimes as feminine, unless the sense of the text requires a precise assignation of gender. So when applied to children please take 'him' and 'his' to include 'her' and 'hers', and vice versa. Similarly, despite having had the privilege of meeting a number of excellent male nursery workers, we have referred throughout to practitioners as 'her'. These arbitrary decisions have been taken in the interests of readability and clarity; if they offend anyone we apologise.

The editors have imposed a certain amount of standardisation on the text, but in general the writers' own preferences for terminology (e.g. 'child-initiated' or 'self-initiated') have been followed. The same with spelling, so that although English spelling rules have been applied throughout, readers will find a few variations (e.g. both 'organise' and 'organize').

Contributors made their own decisions about references and bibliographies. Some have included extensive lists of reference works and recommendations for further reading. Others have made little reference to other authorities and have concentrated on their own reflections based on their own observations and experience. The result is a thorough, thought provoking examination of a vital area of provision. We hope that readers and the children with whom they work will gain from it.

Sally and Phill Featherstone, June 2013

Introduction

Why is there a need for a book on child-initiated learning? It is hoped that this book itself provides the answer, but the need for it was expressed very clearly by a contributor to the Foundation Stage Forum (www.foundation-stage.info)

> *I am a newly returning teacher and … I am finding it hard to understand exactly how child-initiated learning should work. The phrase is clear enough but how do I plan for it? Should I do any planning? Should it be an ongoing feature in the timetable or a separate slot in the day? I feel lost and no one has any answers for my questions at school. Please share with me how you do it and any information will be helpful.*
>
> (posted May 2007)

This practitioner's cry for help is echoed by many, who feel themselves under pressure to provide something they are not sure how to do.

- What's child-initiated learning about?
- Do I make a selection of resources from which I let children choose? Or do I just turn them loose and let them decide what they're going to do?
- If I give them completely free choice, how can I be sure that they're going to be learning? They might end up doing the same thing over and over again, day after day? Does it matter?
- I have a responsibility to plan for progress, so that when the Foundation Stage Profiles are completed and children move into Key Stage 1 they've covered all the ground they're supposed to. Can I take the risk of letting them choose for themselves?
- How much time should I devote to child-initiated learning?

The initial Early Years Foundation Stage documents (DfES 2007) strongly emphasised the desirability of play, child involvement and active learning. These all imply child-initiated activity but, as Jennie Lindon points out later in this book, not much help was given in forming a view of what exactly this is. How should it be defined?

The Framework for the Revised EYFS has defined the relationship between adult-led and child-initiated activities as:

> *Each area of learning and development must be implemented through planned, purposeful play and through a mix of adult-led and child-initiated activity. Play is essential for children's development, building their confidence as they learn to explore, to think about problems, and relate to others.*
>
> *Children learn by leading their own play, and by taking part in play, which is guided by adults. There is an ongoing judgement to be made by practitioners about the balance between activities led by children, and activities led or guided by adults. Practitioners must respond to each child's emerging needs and interests, guiding their development through warm, positive interaction.*
>
> *As children grow older, and as their development allows, it is expected that the balance will gradually shift towards more activities led by adults, to help children prepare for more formal learning, ready for Year 1.*
>
> (Statutory Framework for the Early Years Foundation Stage; Department for Education; 2012)

Definitions are helpful, but still leave room for differences in interpretation. For example, there are those who would argue (and later in this book some do) that a practitioner planning a selection of activities and providing the resources for them, from which the child chooses, although satisfying the above definition is not child-initiated learning in the true sense.

In the above definitions, adult-led and child-initiated are at opposite ends of a spectrum. There is another approach not defined in the guidance. That is, where the adult chooses the activity and provides the resources, but allows the child the scope to use the resources and experience the activity in their own way. At its best this leads to the adult and child working together in a constructive partnership to exploit the learning potential offered by the activity. Some include this way of working under the term 'adult-initiated'.

There is also confusion about the *balance* between child-initiated and adult-directed activities, so that many of those who are confident about what they are doing are not as confident about how much of it they should be doing.

totally
adult-directed
(the Victorian
schoolroom)

totally
child-initiated
(A.S.Neill)

Imagine child activity as a continuum, a line. At one end is the traditional classroom, where for the entire time children are given tasks (often worksheets) to do and all their learning is planned for them. This represents a curriculum which is totally adult-directed, you might say adult dominated. At the opposite end of the line is A.S. Neill's Summerhill, where the regime was such that children were able to make all the decisions about what they did – or even whether they did anything at all. Most people would agree that there's a place for both approaches in moderation, but that neither is desirable on its own. So where on the continuum line is the right balance? The simple answer is that there is no 'right' balance. Individuals (children as well as practitioners) vary. So do settings. What is appropriate for one may not be appropriate for another. And what is appropriate at one time of the week (or year, or day) might not be so at another.

An appreciation of the relationship between 'knowledge', 'skills' and 'understanding' helps to bring child-initiated learning into focus. 'Knowledge' is information, data, what is known. It relates to what things are, how they work, how they behave. 'Skills' are the abilities needed to apply knowledge. 'Understanding' covers the development of the mental concepts and the physical capacities to be able to employ the knowledge and skills. Understanding – almost entirely in children and much of the time in adults – comes about empirically as an outcome of practice. For example, a child might have the knowledge that a pencil will make a mark on paper. In order to make a mark they need the skill and control to be able to hold the pencil and direct it properly. But in order to use the pencil and the paper to convey meaning through a word or a picture they need to experience, to experiment and to practise with the pencil over a period of time. All three of these areas can be and are developed through child-initiated learning. Understanding – perhaps simultaneously the most complex and most crucial of these abilities – is probably least amenable to development through an approach which makes heavy use of adult-directed activities, and where children's enterprise and initiative are reined in.

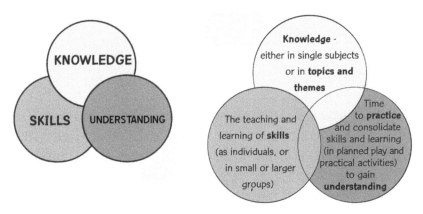

Knowledge, understanding and skills support each other and overlap.

There have been a number of statements in key documents from the DfES (as it then was) about the place of child-initiated activities in the curriculum and their relationship to other approaches. Here are two of the most influential:

> *There should be opportunities for children to engage in activities planned by adults and also those that they plan or initiate themselves. Children do not make a distinction between 'play' and 'work' and neither should practitioners. Children need time to become engrossed, work in depth and complete activities.*
>
> KEEP (Key Elements of Effective Practice);
> *Primary National Strategy* (2005)

'Practitioners should also be aware of the main findings of the Effective Provision of Pre-school Education project (EPPE)6 research.

- *Effective pedagogy is both 'teaching', and the provision of instructive learning environments and routines.*
- *The most effective settings provide both teacher-initiated group work and freely chosen yet potentially instructive play activities.*
- *Excellent settings tend to achieve an equal balance between adult-led and child-initiated interactions and activities.*
- *Cognitive outcomes relate to focused group work planned and initiated by practitioners and the amount of sustained shared thinking between practitioners and children.'*

Developing the foundations for curricular target setting in ISP schools birth to five, DfES 2005

This guidance from the DfES and the Primary National Strategy, which appeared in 2005, was strongly influenced by the Effective Provision of Pre-school Education (EPPE) research, and for the first time gave in writing a view on the balance between child-initiated and adult-directed activities recommended as effective practice in the early years. It recognised that teaching (in its broadest sense, not merely formal instruction), the establishment of routines (which we know give children feelings of security and foster confidence) and a stimulating learning environment are all essential elements for promoting effective learning. It also acknowledged that there was a need for both teacher (practitioner) initiated activities and 'potentially instructive play', and that the balance between adult-led and child-initiated activities should be roughly equal. In other words, an approach which is going to be desirable most of the time and in most cases sits about halfway along the continuum line in the diagram on page ix.

This view was strengthened by guidance issued by the National Assessment Agency in 2006. The point being addressed was how to gather the assessment evidence needed to complete the Foundation Stage Profile, where to look and what 'counted'.

> *When making a judgement ... practitioners should draw on at least 80% of evidence from child-initiated learning, and no more than 20% of evidence from adult-directed or focused assessments.*

In other words, the balance for assessment should very much favour activities chosen and pursued by the child. This confirmed the value of freely chosen 'potentially instructive play' in providing evidence of what a child knows, understands and can do. It of course throws up another list of questions for practitioners, not the least of which is how you make assessments when the children come up with outcomes that are unplanned (by the adult) and unexpected.

OFSTED provides a pointer in this regard, emphasising the importance of talk. In *Getting on well, the second national report on how early years and childcare providers are supporting Every Child Matters outcomes for children*, OFSTED concluded that 'teaching methods to extend children's learning were inconsistent and at times inappropriate'. The action they recommended was to 'develop adults' understanding of how to question children effectively during '... child-initiated activities...' (OFSTED 2007). This highlights another thread which runs through many of the contributions to this book: that is, the importance of children, with the help and encouragement of adults, talking about their activities. Sensitive oral interventions by practitioners will assist children to internalise their experiences, turning experiment and practice into understanding.

The Framework for the Revised EYFS (2012) has been helpful in defining the Characteristics of Effective Learning, and these form the basis for the structure of the Revised Development Matters www.foundationyears.org.uk

Three characteristics of effective teaching and learning are:

- playing and exploring – children investigate and experience things, and 'have a go'
- active learning – children concentrate and keep on trying if they encounter difficulties, and enjoy achievements
- creating and thinking critically – children have and develop their own ideas, make links between ideas, and develop strategies for doing things

Practitioners can now using these characteristics to evaluate their own effectiveness in planning and guiding children's activities.

This book has been conceived and written in response to the issues described above, and in order to answer some of the questions faced by adults who work with (or support those who work with) children under five. A number of experienced early years advisers and writers offer their reflections and ideas on what child-initiated learning is, why it is important, how and where it fits into day-to-day early years provision, and how it can be assessed.

They chose their own topics and wrote about them in the way they wished. This book is the result. We are grateful to them for their participation and for sharing their wisdom.

Bibliography and references

Department for Education (2012), *Statutory Framework for the Early Years Foundation Stage*.

Early Education, for the DFE (2012), *Development Matters in the Early Years Foundation Stage*, www.foundationyears.org.uk

DfES (2005), KEEP (Key Elements of Effective Practice); *Primary National Strategy*. London: DFES.

DfES (2005), *Developing the foundations for curricular target setting in ISP schools, birth to five*. London: DfES.

OFSTED (2007), *Early years: Getting on well – enjoying, contributing and achieving*. London: Office for Standards in Education.

NAA (2006), London: National Assessment Agency (www.standards.dfes.gov.uk/local/eyfs/site/glossary)

Part 1: Starting points and definitions

Jennie Lindon: What does child-initiated learning mean, where does it fit and why is it important for young children?

1

The stage of children's development and learning which precedes entering school and embarking on the National Curriculum has evolved certain principles and a pedagogy which are now widely accepted. Central is an emphasis on play and a recognition of how play contributes to learning.

The Early Years Foundation Stage (EYFS) guidance for England has confirmed the strong focus on play that dominated both the initial guidance for the Foundation Stage and the Birth to Three Matters materials. The EYFS guidance is also consistent with previous documents in the emphasis on a well resourced, easily accessible, indoor and outdoor learning environment. Sensible adult planning is weighted towards creating the favourable circumstances in which young children can easily choose and organise themselves for significant periods of time during their day or session in an early years setting, or in the home of their childminder. The whole ethos of the EYFS remains that children's non-family early years experiences should be relaxed, home-like and led from children's own interests and personal timing. There is no support for school lesson-type planning, nor for a school classroom atmosphere. Early years practice is now guided by a revised, much shorter EYFS framework. The issues in this chapter still apply; they have not been resolved by the Revised EYFS (2012).

The statutory guidance for the EYFS stresses that all seven areas of learning are 'equally important and depend on each other to support a rounded approach to child development. All the areas must be delivered through planned, purposeful play, with a balance of adult-led and child-initiated activities'. The wording of that last sentence creates a number of problems of interpretation. What does 'planned' mean in practice? Does it mean open-ended planning, responsive to what actually happened the previous week or day? Are written plans closed to any further input? Does any plan require certainty about what is going to happen and why? Or is planning respectful of the uncertainty that is an integral part of genuine play for children, not only in their early years? How do we recognise 'purposeful play'? Whose purposes: those of the children or those of the adults? What is meant by 'balance'? Are acceptable purposes defined in advance by adults as pre-determined outcomes for any activities?

We need to think hard about these questions, not only about which answers will support children in their current learning but also about how they will develop their positive disposition to learn in the future and their view of themselves as learners – or not.

There is good reason to support the approach of the playwork profession and argue that proper, playful play (if we need lots of Ps!) is the way that children are enabled to learn what cannot be taught directly by adults. As soon as adults stake a claim on 'play' to fit their own designs and intentions, the word starts to mean something very different. (See Lindon, 2001, for a discussion of the development of an adult-led perspective on 'learning through play'.) But also we must ask another and very crucial question. What is actually meant by the terms 'adult-led' and 'child-initiated'? What do these different approaches look like in practice, in the setting, day by day? Are there different working definitions and, if so, does this change the experience for children?

The discussion needs to start with that final question, because sensible answers to the other questions will evolve from this understanding. The birth to five EYFS guidance has chosen to talk about 'adult-led' rather than 'adult-initiated' experiences. The two phrases do not have the same meaning, and problems can arise for practitioners and teams who find it hard to reflect or who are anxious about possible criticism of their practice. Like the Foundation Stage guidance which preceded it, the EYFS document stresses the importance of a balance between an adult focus and 'child-initiated' experiences. But whether this balance will work for the benefit of children depends a great deal on what is meant by 'child-initiated'.

What should 'child-initiated' mean?

The first printing (2007) of the EYFS materials did not include a definition of child-initiated learning, although the supporting materials, such as the Principles into Practice cards, pointed in the right direction. Definitions were added to the Practice Guidance (page 7) in May 2008, making it very clear that, 'When a child engages in a self-chosen pursuit, this is child-initiated activity'. An example is given of a child who elects to play with a fire engine and determines all the details of that play. The explanation also includes that, '... child-initiated activities may be instigated when a child brings something to the setting – such as an experience of having been on a bus or visiting hospital'. Practitioners may then follow this child's lead by providing suitable resources. Ann Langston, writing in *Nursery World* in late 2007, provided further help. 'When a child (of any age) engages in a self-chosen pursuit we describe this as a child-initiated activity, valuing the child's choice and recognising and respecting the child's purpose'. Langston also introduced the important, and meaningful, idea that '... a child-initiated choice may be where a child takes ownership of an activity and 'subverts' it to a purpose different from that intended'.

The example given is of a child who has had enough of watering the plants with an adult and decides to pour water into a hole to make a puddle. Other child-initiated experiences follow from when a child brings an object of importance into the early years setting or wants to talk about a recent experience. The acceptance that children can take over an adult-initiated experience is also part of the definition given in the revised EYFS guidance.

How is 'child-initiated' sometimes interpreted?

Words matter, and a primary school definition of 'child-initiated' has slid unannounced into some early years thinking. In the more structured primary school day, small windows of choice are sometimes called 'child-initiated time'. Children can choose from resources that are made available for this more flexible slot in the timetable. This development is often a laudable attempt to create a more playful element within the primary school curriculum. Primary school life is more highly organised than the early years – the reason why children's playtime and a well resourced playground are so crucial. But, and it is a major BUT, early years provision is not school. Even the reception class is the last part of the early years stage and not the beginning of the school curriculum. The school model leads to a working definition of 'child-initiated' that includes, as a given, a great deal of adult input. An example of the problem can be found in the Foundation Stage booklet of the *Social and Emotional Aspects of Learning* (SEAL) materials. On page 6, 'adult-led' is defined as 'where language and ideas are specifically introduced and developed by the practitioner'. 'Child-initiated' is described as 'where learning is ... supported by adaptations to the learning environment and social interaction which promote particular avenues of exploration and discussion'. (At the time of writing SEAL is available to download on: www.standards.dfes.gov.uk/primary/publications/banda/seal)

'Initiate' means to begin or start, to enter upon an action or activity, to introduce or set something going, to originate. So to be truly child-initiated, experiences or activities have to be genuinely chosen and organised by children. The additional explanation now in the EYFS Practice Guidance shows that this meaning was what the EYFS development team meant when they used the term. However, when early years practitioners accept the 'primary school' definition described above they open the door for a disruption of early childhood. There is a high risk that young children will be made to relinquish vital experiences in favour of a life-by-lesson-plan approach. The EYFS stresses the great importance of 'learning through play', but are children's play choices only acceptable if they are tidied up, controlled and 'pre-schooled' by adults?

Developmentally appropriate experiences during early childhood let babies, toddlers and children develop at their own pace. When young children have what they deserve – the time to explore, communicate, repeat and revisit – they are poised, at five to six years of age, to manage the more structured primary school day. However, they are best prepared for that different kind of experience by being allowed to be young children, certainly not by being categorised as 'pre-schoolers'. Indeed, the best primary school practice now aims to extend a child-focused early years approach into the first years of statutory education.

A serious problem has now developed. Some materials written for early years practitioners include under the heading 'child-initiated' suggestions which actually require a great deal of adult pre-planning and direction. Readers are given guidance on how particular materials should be laid out, and how children should be encouraged to undertake specific actions with these materials and follow adult determined extensions to the activity. These suggestions are made with specific ends in mind, and are often accompanied by a list of comments adults should make and suitable questions to ask the children – all this before children have yet got their hands on the materials!

Some of these ideas are constructive and can be a valuable addition to adult input – so long as they are seen as a resource on which to draw, rather than a to-do list. However, the key point is that it is impossible to see how children will have originated any of the experiences which follow from them. The suggestions may be less directive than those given under the heading 'adult-led', but by following them practitioners introduce a pre-determined collection of resources, and it is they, not the children, who set going and determine the direction of the questions and the exploration.

An easy to-and-fro between who leads and who initiates

The findings of the Effective Provision of Pre-School Education (EPPE) research are a reliable guide to what 'child-initiated' has to mean for early years provision. This research influenced the EYFS and is loosely quoted by politicians as evidence that early years provision leads to measurable benefits for children. However, the EPPE research did not rubber-stamp just any early years provision. The team looked at the details of what needed to happen as part of high quality experiences for children in non-family settings. (The project mainly observed and assessed children over the age of three.) A crucial finding was that best practice to support young learning was created through a balance in the days in favour of child-initiated experiences over those initiated by adults. The finding is often quoted as supporting a 50:50 ratio between adult and child-initiated activities, but the actual recommendation is that the balance should be more like 3:2 in favour of child-initiated learning.

Interestingly, the EPPE team did not formally define 'child-initiated' because they judged that the meaning was obvious! However, the research papers show that the EPPE project took an interpretation similar to the one I have offered above. The team often use the words 'freely chosen' to underline that good practice requires children to be able to select, without adult direction, from a well-resourced learning environment. An equally important finding was that children's learning was supported best when practitioners felt confident to come alongside children, to be attentive, respond to direct questions from children and add their own adult comments. Examples from the research papers show ways in which the contributions of adults were directly relevant to the play or conversation. Sometimes practitioners offered a possibility (not a requirement) to extend play through a suggestion or question. Sometimes they encouraged children to think and wonder, because the adult did not give a 'right' answer.

The EPPE team called this mutually supportive communication a process of 'sustained shared thinking'. Adult communication was led by attention to the immediate evidence of their ears and eyes and not by a list of 'questions I prepared earlier'. Nor did the genuinely supportive adults seize control of enthusiastic child conversations or play sequences and drive down the SEAL route of pre-prepared 'avenues of exploration'. The EPPE team ascribes the value of adult-initiated experiences to promoting a role for adults in which they contribute their greater general knowledge and experience of engaging activities.

The words and actions needed to sustain shared thinking come about through carefully considered adult-initiated experiences that may also be adult-led, at least at the outset. However, good early years practice allows for a flow, and adult-initiated and adult-led activities should allow plenty of scope for children to share the control and make choices about how to use materials, timing and conversation, and most definitely about what, if anything, emerges as a tangible end product. Marion Dowling (2005) has developed visual materials that help to bring alive the concept of sustained shared thinking. Adult-initiated or led experiences that work for young children are offered by practitioners who are able to live with the uncertainty that lies at the core of genuine play. Conversation happens because children want to talk and listen and because the practitioners look keen to hear and to behave as proper conversational partner – not like someone who you would dread having sit next to you on a long train journey!

Child-initiated experiences

We can summarise the definition offered earlier by saying that child-initiated activities and events arise when children choose freely from their learning environment – indoors and out – and select and organise resources, picking their own companions on the way. Babies pull the basket of scarves towards them and toddlers take a book off the low shelf. Older toddlers and two year-olds organise their dolls and pile bricks into a large basket. Three, four and five year-olds select a simple board or card game or organise their own outdoor book corner. They decide that their shop needs sorting out, they play chase or return to a long running pretend-play narrative. Some experiences are totally led and directed by the children, and adults may not be required or involved at all.

Sometimes you will be close by, able to see and hear what happens in the play. These opportunities often provide good examples to extend your understanding of what individual children comprehend and how they use their skills and knowledge. The EYFS emphasises that useful observations of children are weighted towards their spontaneous play and the free flow of their interests, and counsels against assuming that observations are only made when an activity has been planned by the adults. This is supported by the 2006 guidance from the National Assessment Agency (NAA), which recommends that no more than 20% of the assessment evidence should come from adult-directed activities and the remaining 80% or more from observations of activities children have initiated themselves.

Young children are able to make real decisions about play when early years practitioners give priority to providing indoor and outdoor learning environments which allow access to a broad range of resources and opportunities. One of the four strands within the EYFS highlights the importance of 'enabling environments'. Good early years practice leaves plenty of scope for children to find and choose play materials and to move them to where they need them for their play. This rich learning environment can and should be carried through into reception classes in schools – indeed, I have seen it in action. Reception teams who truly care about learning hold tight to the right balance between child and adult-initiated experiences and take care to be clear about who leads when. See, for example, the account provided by Liz Marsden and Jenny Woodbridge (2005).

Planning which focuses on the learning environment means that the pressure on adults is lifted. There is no point or value in trudging wearily through daily activity/ toy/play plans, when a well-provided indoor and outdoor environment invites children by offering accessible, permanently available play resources. See for example the advice from the LEARN team (2002) and Community Playthings (2005). Practitioners then need only to consider one or two special experiences or opportunities for the day, which children can join in, or not, as they wish. Any special, small group coming-together time is led through the key person system and with a careful eye on how it works for children. The overall goal is that children are enabled to learn, and moreover to enjoy, their day in the setting. The main point must never be to complete the written plan just because it's there, regardless of children's lack of enthusiasm.

When adults join child-initiated experiences

You may become involved in child-initiated experiences in two main ways. As a familiar adult, the children will invite (indeed sometimes order) you to get involved in their jigsaw, be a customer in their café, hold this hoop or help them find the snails. Babies and toddlers make it very clear that you are to play peek-a-boo right now, or that this book or that song would be a very good idea. The other route to involvement is when you come alongside children's play, join in and make appropriate comments – about what you and they are doing in the sand or with the farm animals. Your language and your play build on what is happening in front of you. Consequently, you and the children have a good chance of sharing the same reference point. Genuinely helpful practitioners do not take over children's play, either by actions or by intrusive questioning. Elizabeth Wood (2006) puts it well when she describes the role of the adult as being a 'co-player' with children.

Early years practitioners are attentive to individual children. So you will be aware of the ways in which temperament, experiences or the impact of disability can affect them. Decision making should not be a burden for children. Some girls and boys may be made anxious by choice, and they will need and want more direction from you. So, it is not adult interference if you make a gentle suggestion, by words or your own play actions, or if you simplify choice for a child who shows signs of becoming overwhelmed.

The EPPE research described how, in the best early years settings re-viewed, practitioners became involved in about half of the episodes of child-initiated play and conversation. Adults extend young development by showing respect for children's current interests and preferred ways of learning. The adult role can be anything from very close involvement, through attentiveness rom a distance, to being mainly uninvolved in this play because the children are busy out of your obvious sight and hearing. The physical boundaries to your provision should be safe, so that you can allow older children the freedom to move and wander that their play requires. It goes without saying that babies and young toddlers will not be out of your sight unless they are safely asleep.

Reflect on adult-initiated or adult-led experiences

There can be an assumption that children learn only when adults set out deliberately to tell or show them something. This is clearly not the case, and it is positively unhelpful to children's learning if practitioners divide up the day rigidly into 'structured' activities, led by the adults and separate from 'free play'. This approach is often accompanied by the assumption, conveyed in countless subtle ways, that the former is more important than the latter, characterised by a regime in which young children must 'do their work' before they are 'allowed to play'. It is a negative message, if tolerance of very structured tasks is the price children must pay to get out into the garden or be allowed to return to their pretend-play narrative.

An additional, and very serious, problem with activities that are over prescribed by adults is that the practice is dragged further and further away from authentic, hands-on experiences for children. Diane Rich *et al* (2005) documented their alternative approach after seeing many children complete topics in which they had minimal contact with the real thing. One example included a topic on fruit when no fruit of any kind was available. Jacqui Cousins' observations (1999) document how children's busy learning and concentration can be disrupted when practitioners cannot see beyond their own written plan and related outcomes. She describes four-year-olds whose creative explorations and thoughtful conversations were regularly interrupted by having to complete worksheets.

An inviting and appealing activity will have children clustered around you, like bees round a honey pot. There is something awry with the activity, the adult's approach, or both if children need to be dragooned into taking part. There is something wrong if you are stalking children with a clipboard of names, to ensure that everyone has completed their coloured-in ladybird, currant bun or whatever is today's required end product. Stop and reflect on why you are doing this. What are the children actually learning from it? The escapees who persistently drift away are definitely learning something, as are the 'daub and dash' children, who rush through what they have to do in order to complete it in the minimum time and get on to something that interests them more. But their learning is not positive – more a case of 'adults are very boring, run and hide!'

Go back to the basics: What were you hoping children would learn from what you had planned? How else could they learn it? Is it possible that they are in fact learning successfully through their freely chosen play and you have not noticed? Perhaps someone, sometime, has led you to believe that learning only counts if it fits the list that adults predicted earlier. A rigid model, driven by prescribed outcomes, has the capacity to seriously disrupt good quality learning experience – not just during the EYFS but in the school years as well.

Of course, the tightly defined objectives and their associated checklist are a security mechanism which some practitioners feel forced on them by the need to account for progress. Some, too, genuinely believe that the most effective way to be sure that children are achieving stated learning objectives is to create tasks, the completion of which will allow them to tick off criteria as having been met. This provides the required proof that the children have learnt. EYFS documentation is clear that the dominant method of assessing achievement and progress should be looking at what children are doing. So observing, noting descriptive anecdotes and taking photos of any experiences that absorb children should provide all the assessment evidence you will need for young children. For good examples of how well this can work, see the use of photos to tell a learning story brought together by Carmel Brennan (2004). Look also at the explanation of the Learning Journey in the EYFS CD-ROM under the Principles into Practice card 3.1.

The expectations of parents are another factor which can mitigate against a child led, free play approach. The assumption is that parents will doubt their child is 'learning' unless they have daily, tangible evidence of it: the coloured-in ladybird, the currant bun, the collage. This is compounded by the responsibility the practitioner feels to treat all children fairly and equally and to ensure that no one misses out by going home empty handed. But you can show and share in many ways. Is it wise for you, as a practitioner, to submit yourself to being judged on how much 'paperwork' a child produces? Or on whether or not a child has something to take home at the end of the day? Some children will be without a ladybird, currant bun or whatever, but how much does that matter? Lack of ladybirds is only a problem if you make a display with named items that suggests every child should have produced one that day. If you are cooking with children, make some extra buns to share with the children who have not cooked. If children are genuinely sad because they have missed an activity they now realise might have been fun, do it again tomorrow!

There are some other issues of practice that involve tougher reflection and maybe the need for additional support. If you are honest, does the problem lie in you yourself, because you find it difficult to let go? Do you feel uneasy about sharing control of the day with children? Try letting go a little at a time. Chaos will not follow. Or is it that someone else is the source of problems? Many early years leaders are supportive and insightful, but some run their setting as if it were a medieval fiefdom, with their staff as the peasants. It can be very difficult for practitioners to develop their own good practice, because they are told what to do and no deviation from the leader's written plan is tolerated. If there is no room to exercise professional judgement or for discussion, practitioners have little option but to seek the help of others – the management committee or the early years advisory team for the area.

Enjoyable adult-initiated and adult-led experiences

It is not intended to suggest that activities and experiences initiated or led by adults are inferior or unenjoyable. Good quality early learning requires adults who have plenty of ideas of their own, but who are also sensitive to what enthuses or puzzles an individual child on a particular day. Adult-initiated activities are pre-planned (but not over planned) and started by adults. But the experience planned by the practitioner is offered to children along with real choice about their degree of involvement and how the experiences will unfold.

One approach is to put out some interesting materials and begin to play with them yourself. These materials may be unfamiliar to the children, or they could be a resource that comes back fresh because it is not available all the time. You might start the play with some musical instruments, a different way of mark-making or a story bag. Children will notice what you are doing and become curious. They will begin to take an interest. If they start to get engaged with the resource you can slowly withdraw and let them take over the activity. Good practice is to be an interested play companion and allow children to control the final directions. The degree of their interest determines whether an enjoyable experience needs to be extended by giving it more time and space, or by repeating it very soon.

Sometimes adults will initiate and lead or direct an activity because the resources are unfamiliar or because less experienced children need to be guided and perhaps shown safe techniques, for example in cooking or woodwork. Other enjoyable activities simply will not work without friendly adult direction. For instance, young children may need help with musical activities or understanding how to use a piece of equipment or play a game. After all, they cannot ask to do something again until they have experienced it at least once already.

In good early years practice, there continues to be a flow between these different kinds of experiences. When adult-led or adult-initiated activities seize children's interest, then they start to shape what happens next. When adults are invited into children's play, ideas often evolve for appropriate adult-initiated experiences, or the fine tuning of flexible adult plans for next week. It may not be obvious to a visitor who started what, until you and the children explain. The examples documented by the Curiosity and Imagination project (2005) show the to-and-fro of shared control and ideas when practitioners truly work together with children in a creative enterprise that is allowed to take its time.

Some of the adult-initiated and adult-led activities will be spontaneous, not pre-planned at all. Alert practitioners are ready to seize the moment and make suggestions: 'Let's run round the garden!' or 'Who wants to water our tomatoes?' Some experiences, such as local trips, will need to be organised in advance. An adult leads and guides a visit to the park, but what happens when you get there should be shaped just as much by the children. Be flexible. Young children can be very firm about the 'proper route' for walking to the library, or can insist that no market trip is complete without buying some fruit from their favourite stall.

With an appropriate balance children will have an enjoyable childhood, rich in active learning. They will stock up fine memories, and supportive practitioners will have satisfying and stimulating days with their young companions. The reward is to feel and to know that you are making a positive difference. And by the by, you will also be following the guidance within the national early years frameworks, including the Early Years Foundation Stage for England.

Bibliography and references

Brennan, C. (ed.) (2004), *Power of play: a play curriculum in action*. Dublin: IPPA.

Community Playthings (2005), *Creating places for birth to threes – room layout and equipment*. See also www. communityplaythings.co.uk

Cousins, J. (1999), *Listening to four year olds: how they can help us plan their education and care*. London: National Children's Bureau.

Inspiring Creativity and Imagination (2005) download www.surestart.gov.uk/communications/childcare workers/inspiringcreativity

Early Education, for the DFE (2012), *Development Matters in the Early Years Foundation Stage*, www. foundationyears.org.uk

Dowling, Marion. (2005), *Supporting young children's sustained shared thinking: an exploration* (book and DVD). London: Early Education.

EPPE (Effective Provision of Pre-School Education Project) reports and papers on www.ioe.ac.uk/schools/ ecpe/eppe

REPEY (Researching Effective Pedagogy in Early Years) www.dfes.gov.uk/research/data/uploadfiles/RB356. doc

Langston, Ann. (2007), 'All about the language of the EYFS' in *Nursery World*, 1 November 2007. London: Haymarket Publications.

London Borough of Lewisham (2002), *A place to learn: developing a stimulating environment*. London: LEARN.

Lindon, Jennie. (2001), *Understanding Children's Play*. Cheltenham: Nelson Thornes.

—(2012), *Understanding child development 0-8 years: linking theory and practice*. London: Hodder Arnold.

Lindon, Jennie and Lindon, Lance (2011), *Leadership and Early Years Professionalism*. London: Hodder Education.

Marsden, L. and Woodbridge, J. (2005), *Looking closely at learning and teaching… a journey of development*. Huddersfield: Early Excellence.

Rich, Diane *et al.* (2005), *First hand experience: what matters to children*. Rich Learning Opportunities.

Wood, E. (2006) 'The value of Child-initiated learning' and 'How to support child-initiated learning' in *Practical Pre-School*, September 2006, issue 67. London: Step Forward Publishing.

The ideas in this chapter are my own and I take responsibility for the views expressed. However, I have appreciated conversations with professional colleagues while I was working to understand what had happened to key definitions, and the sense of pressure and anxiety felt by a number of early years practitioners. Wendy Russell's ideas around the uncertainty of genuine play and practitioners' feelings about control have been very useful. I learned a great deal from my time with the *What Matters to Children* team. I am grateful to Iram Siraj-Blatchford for several conversations about the EPPE/REPEY research.

Linda Pound: Playing what you know

2

The traditions of early childhood education have emphasised both the importance of building on children's interests and enthusiasms and the value of play. The dissenting voices of politicians and journalists and some parents suggest that these factors are too soft and woolly, and true learning requires a commitment to formal objectives addressed through structured tasks, thoroughly planned in advance. However, developmental psychology and neuroscience have done much to strengthen the views of those who continue to argue that the best way to inspire, support and strengthen learning is by enabling children to start and shape activities which arise from the things that interest them because they are important in their own lives: in other words, child-initiated learning.

The revised EYFS (Dfe 2012) has for the first time made the *how* of teaching and learning statutory. For the first time practitioners are *required* to ensure that the following are addressed:

- playing and exploration
- active learning
- creating and thinking critically

In short, a focus on what children are learning is no longer enough – playing what you know and what you are to learn becomes an essential part of practice.

In this chapter I am going to argue that children become expert through play, and that the best way for practitioners to help children achieve learning success is by engineering opportunities for them to hone, refine and order their interests through play which they have initiated themselves. Susan Greenfield, a celebrated neuroscientist, writes of play as 'fun with serious consequences' (1996: 75). I want us to consider what those consequences are.

Play is the natural activity of the child, common across all cultures. But, like language and music, it is culturally influenced. That is to say that we are all born with a propensity to play (or talk or make music) but whether and how we do these things will depend on what happens around us. From their earliest days, babies begin to learn about aspects of play. They develop their skills of and expertise in play, and as they do so adults find ways to help them connect and communicate with the world around them – through language, music, gesture and facial expression.

Playfulness starts early. Babies and toddlers enjoy finding ways to engage the adults around them by making them laugh (Trevarthen 1998). Adults, in the songs they use, the games they play and the gentle teasing of games such as Peek-a-Boo and Round and Round the Garden, draw children into the playful world that will support their learning throughout life. Baby play is immediate, the reward enjoyment. But as children learn to think and to manipulate objects their play takes on a more experimental dimension. The development of imaginative play allows children to explore, practise, hypothesise and predict – in short to make sense of the world.

Adults, too, enjoy the play of small children. Look at the pleasure the new parent gets from tickling a baby, or the fun in playing hide and find with a small child. By supporting children in learning to play, adults can and do influence their interests, through the opportunities for play they provide and by the ways in which they demonstrate and involve children in their own interests. But in the end, the content and focus of their play – the issues which they seek to make sense of – can only be determined by the children themselves.

These interests or enthusiasms have rightly been called 'imperatives'. Let us take an example of an imperative in action. Three-year-old Max was into transporting. He cruised the nursery riding a dumper truck. First he filled the scoop with books. Practitioners vetoed that idea and helped him to put the books back on the shelves. Next he raided the home corner and filled the scoop with dolls, blankets and dishes. Well-meaning staff persuaded him that other children were using those things, so off he scooted again. Blocks, farm animals and crayons all got the same response from the adults. Later in the morning, Max was observed driving as close to the walls as he could and carefully picking up tiny pieces of dust and fluff that he discovered along the edge of the skirting board. At last he had found something to transport! Children motivated by a particular schema will go to great lengths to explore the interest that is driving them.

Children's interests will probably be closely linked to their biological or developmental needs. At around a year old, for example, babies are driven to climb – chairs, shelves, steps – anything they can get to. But alongside enthusiasms of this sort, there are many that arise from the culture within which the child grows up.

Forgotten languages

Where do children's interests come from? What originates and perpetuates them? Let us begin by looking at some of the influences which are absorbed unconsciously.

Children's interests reflect the enormous, universal issues and preoccupations which are the substance of myths and fairy tales. These have been referred to by Erich Fromm (1951) as the 'forgotten language'. Like play, dreams and traditional stories allow us to explore puzzling events and phenomena, and to try to interpret them and relate them to our own circumstances. Penny Holland's (2003) work on the role of superheroes in children's play reminds us that children are constantly seeking to understand the themes of death, birth and rebirth which underpin all cultures.

Children are consumers, and the worldwide market for children's toys is worth many millions. There is a constant pressure on parents from the pester factor which is stimulated by a barrage of advertising. Many people worry about the impact of commerce and the influence commercial factors have on children's play and interests. While this cannot be ignored and should not be underestimated, it can be helpful to look beyond the props that children choose – the ubiquitous capes and other paraphernalia, the weapons they create – and think about the imperatives which drive their interest. Egan, in his work on the role of story in learning and teaching (1988), refers to the 'binary opposites' (like birth and death) that preoccupy children. In superhero play children seek to explore opposites that impinge on their daily lives, such as strength and weakness, power and powerlessness. Their play reflects the logic of what Fromm has called 'the one universal language the human race has ever developed' (1951: 7), namely myths and fairy tales.

It would be impossible to leave this aspect of children's interests without some mention of the part played by gender. A government document on boys' achievement (DCSF 2007) underlines the value of exploring children's interests, even when that interest appears to conflict with the values of adults. It is far from clear whether boys and girls behave differently and develop different interests as a result of their biology, generations of role modelling, or because of influences mediated through their immediate environment. It is probably a mixture of all of these, and maybe more. As Rogoff (2003) reminds us:

> *Many heated arguments are based on peoples' views of how things should be as well as on observations of existing gender differences. Although the biological preparation argument and the gender role training argument are*

often put in opposition, they need not be. Indeed, it is difficult to imagine that they do not operate in concert in some way.

Paley (1984, cited by Holland, 2003) links these aspects:

If I have not yet learned to love Darth Vader, I have at least made some useful discoveries while watching him at play. As I interrupt less, it becomes clear that boys' play is serious drama, not morbid mischief. Its rhythms and images are often discordant to me, but I must try to make sense of a style that, after all, belongs to half the population of the classroom.

Cultural memories

Picture the scene. It is Easter Sunday in Malta. The streets are crowded with people of all ages, including babies, youths, adults, parents and great-grandmas. Everyone wears new clothes and an air of excitement. Bands play. Swags of bunting hang from lamp posts and loop between the buildings on either side of the street. Confetti falls like snow from first floor windows. Through the crowded streets a group of men are running. They are carrying between them a large, ornate and heavy statue of a triumphant Christ risen from the dead. After running perhaps 50 yards, cheered on by the crowd and accompanied by lively music, the men raise the statue high above their heads. More confetti is showered on them. There's a short rest and the process is repeated again. And again. And again. Sometimes up and down steps, sometimes taking in steep hills. Eventually the whole circuit of the town is completed and the statue is returned to its place in the cathedral.

During this extended ceremony, young children – far too young to understand the historical basis, let alone the spiritual significance of such an event – are lifted high on the shoulders of adults, bounced in time with the music and included in all the manifestations of pleasure and excitement which surge through the crowd. Although they don't understand the reasons for all the noise and excitement, they are drinking in the importance of this event – hearing the sounds, seeing the movement and colours and feeling the emotion.

In both childhood and adulthood we learn things that we think are important, or that people who are important to us think are important. Levitin (2007) reminds us that:

Memory strength (or learning) is also a function of how much we care about the experience. Neurochemical tags associated with memories mark them of importance, and we tend to code as important things that carry with them a lot of emotion, either positive or negative.

It is surely the empirical evidence of these effects which has led societies to develop shared experiences of ritual, whether they be weddings, football matches, pop concerts, state occasions or religious ceremonies. Cultural events to which we have been introduced in early childhood remain important to us throughout our lives because of the emotional and sensory experiences involved in the memories they carry. We probably do not even know why – but the sound of a particular kind of music, a taste, a smell, or the sight of confetti carried in the breeze can stir strong emotions and responses. The brains of the children watching the festival in Malta will be busily coding their experiences as important.

Emotional memories and child-initiated play

Memories of this sort are so powerful because they are laid down deep within the brain and have strong emotional markers. Large scale happenings are, of course, not the only cultural experiences which impact on children. Some smaller scale but equally memorable events provide material for children's play. Playing weddings, for example, is a common theme – even amongst those children who have never been to one. Meek (1985) describes a young child's preoccupation with funerals. She had lost a sibling, and she repeatedly played out the ceremony of the funeral. None of the other children had attended a funeral, and some had only a sketchy notion of what one was. Yet she was able to engage other children in her playing out of an event which for her had had a big emotional impact. Four-year-old Isabel, with two younger and demanding siblings, explored in her play around Christmas the demands made on baby Jesus by his mother and father. Two-year-old Marie, given a wooden cake with wooden candles for her birthday, spent hours dividing and re-assembling the cake, replacing the candles and sharing out the 'cake' with anyone who would join in.

Children reflect these early memories in their play. The significance of cultural events becomes the subject of their play as they revisit and process their experiences on the route to making sense of their world. This will include wider cultural events such as birthdays and religious celebrations, but it will also involve significant factors in smaller cultural groups, such as things that are of importance within a particular community or family.

What you care about is what you get good at

There is increasing evidence to support the view that children's interests emerge and develop not only as a result of biology, although biology may have a part to play, but also and perhaps even more importantly as a result of their exposure to the interests and enthusiasms of the adults who are significant in their lives. It was often claimed that Mozart, for example, possessed high musical ability because he came from a musical family and therefore music was in his genes. However, psychologists now emphasise that high achievement is also and probably at least as often the result of long hours of engagement or practice. That Mozart came from a musical family meant not only that he may have possessed genetic factors which predisposed him towards musical achievement but also that in his formative years he was surrounded by significant adults who themselves were highly skilled musicians and for whom music was important. He may have possessed innate ability, but 'Even Mozart had to put in the hours' (Pound and Harrison 2003, citing Mihill).

More recent work underlines the fact that in order to be an expert in anything it is necessary to devote a huge amount of effort and time, estimated to be as much as 10,000 hours. Levitin (2007) writes:

> In study after study, of composers, basketball players, fiction writers, ice skaters, concert pianists, chess players, master criminals, and what have you, this number comes up again and again. Ten thousand hours is equivalent to roughly three hours a day, or twenty hours a week, of practice over ten years ... The ten-thousand-hours theory is consistent with what we know about how the brain learns. Learning requires the assimilation and consolidation of information in neural tissue. The more experiences we have with something, the stronger the memory/learning trace for that experience becomes.

The problem with practice is that unless it is something the individual really wants to do it is difficult to maintain sufficient motivation to find the time and give the attention needed. You have only to think about a baby learning to walk to see how true this is. A baby could never put in the hours and hours of practice required unless they themselves wanted to do it. The sheer effort of getting up and falling down over and over and over again could not be demanded of them; they can only do it because they have chosen to. And an important influence on them choosing to is because that is what the significant adults around them do.

John Sloboda (1994, cited by Pound and Harrison, 2003) studied expert musicians and found five common factors in the early stages of their lives. They had all had a great deal of musical stimulation, long periods of time practising or engaging in musical activity, a focus on having fun with music-making, strong support from family members, who were by no means all experienced or accomplished musicians, and encouragement and opportunities for emotional engagement in and responses to music.

The importance of being an expert

It has been suggested (Inagaki, 1992, cited by Pound and Gura, 1997) that becoming very good in one area allows children to develop the understanding and dispositions necessary to become accomplished in other areas. In Inagaki's study, children became expert at keeping goldfish but their enthusiasm for their pets enabled them to learn how to develop expertise in and enthusiasm for many other things. We have all seen this in those enviable individuals who epitomise the renaissance ideal of the polymath by being good at many things – academic work, games, social relationships, you name it.

The young expert mathematicians who are described by Gifford (2005, citing Young-Loveridge) were most likely to come from families where they discussed numbers and time, money and dates, and where card and dice games were popular. Gifford (2005) describes some of the young experts' unique interests and abilities:

> *One child collected the money in poker games at family gatherings. Another child was very interested in car speeds, time and distance: his family moved frequently and often discussed car journeys ... Seth, whose father kept pigeons ... (had) conversations about racing, time and distance ... A shopkeeper's daughter played at writing long lists of numbers and adding them up. One child with asthma learned to count 30 puffs with her nebulizer. Another knew the weight in kilos of all the members of her family: her mother went to a slimming club and her baby brother was weighed at the clinic ...*

The implications for practitioners

Children's experiences in every aspect of their lives influence what they choose to play, explore and engage with. The connections they make may be everyday ones. Two-year-old Archie, for example, loves machines. His father operates a big strimmer and has a power saw, and these interests are widely reflected in his play. Four-year-old Faith loves mermaids and her play around underwater life has influenced and perhaps driven her enthusiasm for swimming. There are strong arguments that these interests are cosmic in their scope. Vivian Gussin Paley (1988) has described children's core curriculum as fairness, fantasy and friendship. Observing children's interests enables the sensitive practitioner to respond positively and imaginatively to what the child has chosen to do. When we allow children to initiate play we gain a window on their thinking. In observing what they do and what motivates them we gain insights which allow us to construct menus of experiences which will support and extend their interests, helping them to become expert and to learn more effectively.

Observing children's self-initiated activity also enables practitioners to question the traditional divide between work and play. Four-year-old Zac loves to write. At home he composes letters to family members unaided. His mother regularly works from home and for him, writing is (or was) a cultural act. At school, there is little time or space to reflect or make choices. Zac and his classmates are directed from one activity to another, and Zac is beginning to resent the requirement to write. This has affected his enthusiasm for writing at home – he has observed the distinction made by practitioners between work and play. His experience is leading him to form the conclusion that play is what you want to do and work is what you have to do.

Society has an ambivalent attitude to play. On the one hand playing music and playing tennis are not regarded as effortless or lazy occupations. Yet play of itself is often seen as unnecessary. The statutory focus on play as an integral part of effective practice (DfE 2012) may help to change perceptions of its role in learning and development. Allowing children's natural propensity to play to shape their learning will enable them to become expert and to think critically and creatively. They will not merely be playing what they know but coming to know and learn what they play.

Bibliography and references

Department for Education (DfE) (2012), *Statutory Framework for the Early Years Foundation Stage: Setting the standards for learning, development and care for children from birth to five* www.foundationyears.org. uk or www.education.gov.uk

DCSF (2007), *Confident, capable and creative: supporting boys' achievements*. London: Department for Children, Schools & Families.

Egan, K. (1988), *Teaching as Storytelling*. London: Routledge.

Fromm, E. (1951), *The Forgotten Language*. NewYork: Grove Weidenfeld.

Gifford, S. (2005), *Teaching Mathematics 3-5: developing learning in the foundation stage*. Maidenhead: Open University Press.

Greenfield, S. (1996), *The Human Mind Explained*. London: Cassell.

Holland, P. (2003), *We don't play with guns here*. Maidenhead: Open University Press.

Levitin, D. (2007), *This is your Brain on Music – understanding a human obsession*. London: Atlantic Books.

Meek, M. (1985), 'Play and paradoxes: some consideration of imagination and language' in Wells, G. and Nicholls, J. (eds) *Language and learning: an interactional perspective*. London: Falmer Press.

Paley, V. G. (1988), *Bad Guys don't have Birthdays*. Chicago: University of Chicago Press.

Pound, L. and Gura, P. (1997), 'Communities of Experts' in Gura, P. (ed) *Reflections on early education and care*. London: BAECE.

Pound, L. and Harrison, C. (2003), *Supporting Musical Development in the Early Years*. Buckingham: Open University Press.

Rogoff, B. (2003), *The Cultural Nature of Human Development*. Oxford: Oxford University Press.

Trevarthen, C. (1998), 'The child's need to learn a culture' in Woodhead, M. *et al* (eds) *Cultural Worlds of Early Childhood*. London: Routledge/ Open University.

3 Janet Moyles: Empowering children and adults: play and child-initiated learning

As the time of writing, our expectations of young children are currently undergoing yet another upheaval brought about by the implementation of the latest Early Years Foundation Stage (DfE, 2012). Whilst the early years field at large states its belief in the value of play in the early years, the word features only marginally in the new legislation and policy document. Just one paragraph (1.9) outlines the importance of play:

> *'Play is essential for children's development ... children learn by leading their own play, and by taking part in play which is guided by adults.'* (p.6).

Even here, the emphasis is on adult guidance which, on the whole, will normally mean that children do not see the activity as play unless they have initiated and guided it themselves. (For a discussion on different types of child-initiated and adult-initiated learning and play, see Moyles, 2010).

Synonymous with the concept of play has evolved the term 'child-initiated' or 'child-led' learning which stems (according to Kwon 2003) from our English liberal tradition of valuing individual rights through a focus on independence and autonomy. But it also has its basis in social-constructivist theories of learning such as those espoused by Vygotsky (1978) and Rogoff (1998). In the last ten years, findings from the Effective Provision of Preschool Education project (EPPE) have shown that 'sustained shared thinking' – in other words, playing alongside children and sharing equally in their explicit thinking – has added another dimension to ideas about child-initiated learning (see Moyles, 2006; Wyse and Goswami, 2009; Broadhead *et al.*, 2010).

I think practitioners would probably agree that play and the child's individual development and competence are fundamental tenets of early years education and care. At the same time, the pressures are on practitioners to ensure that these behaviours we currently call 'play' and 'child-initiated learning' result in the teaching and learning of literacy and numeracy skills to levels which many feel to be inadvisable and unachievable for our youngest children (see OpenEYE 2007 available at http:// openeyecampaign.wordpress.com and Moyles 2006).

This chapter attempts to explore briefly the theoretical and practical relationships between play and child-initiated learning in an endeavour to enhance understanding of the concepts and issues. After examining the similarities and differences between play and child-initiated learning, I will move on to consider the nature of play and learning provision and the role of practitioners, particularly within current English policy and legislation.

Similarities and differences

It is very difficult to define the concept of play. It has been likened to bubbles which, once grasped, disappear. This suggests something very transitory but, in fact, as I have argued elsewhere (Moyles 2005), bubbles leave a residue. So it is with play – it is almost impossible to 'capture' but observation of children at play will show clearly what they can already do and understand. As Susan Greenfield (2002) explains:

> *Everything children do will leave its mark on the brain. Everything you subsequently see is interpreted in the light of what you've already seen. As you grow, everything is filtered through the checks and balances of pre-existing experiences. We each evaluate the world in a different way, through our own individual experiences.*

Play constitutes this process of 'doing': it is (as Vygotsky, 1976, insists) 'the source of development and creates the zone of proximal development ... The child moves forward essentially through play activity'. Definition is impossible because play is a process – just like learning – a continuum of diverse experiences, behaviours and opportunities from which we gradually become more knowledgeable, skilled and capable. It encompasses every aspect of a child's development – social, emotional, intellectual and physical, in the broadest terms. Play is closely linked with metacognition – our ability to understand our own thinking and thought processes. For this reason, practitioners should talk genuinely to children during their play – that is, engage in dialogue about the play theme or context, not simply leave it to the children or engage in endless questioning.

Play is about observing, looking, listening, touching, tasting, smelling, manipulating, speculating, theorizing, experimenting and creating knowledge and skills. It is also about learning how to learn and to be a learner, and having the ability to cope with not knowing for long enough for knowledge and understanding to become established. This latter is one of the major arguments for play; we must all be able to cope with working on a challenge, otherwise we get too frustrated and disheartened and give up! Play allows children to undertake something without loss of self-esteem and to problem-solve in an open-ended and exploratory way. In this way, it is highly motivational and enables children to develop life-long dispositions and flexible approaches to learning. Several research-based reports into developmental psychology (e.g. POST Report, 2000; Whitebread, 2010; Sheridan *et al.,* 2010) indicate that children's main sensory, cognitive and linguistic growth is developed through play, exploration, talk and interaction with others rather than with systematic instruction.

One of my favourite descriptions of play as a process is that given many years ago now by Pugmire-Stoy (1991) who argues:

'In play, a child accomplishes many things:

- experiments with people and things
- stores information in his/her memory
- studies causes and effects
- reasons out problems
- builds a useful vocabulary
- learns to control self-centred emotional reactions and impulses
- adapts behaviours to the cultural habits of his/her social group
- interprets new and, on occasion, stressful events
- increases ... ideas about self-concept
- develops fine and gross motor skills'

To these, I would also add:

- makes choices
- uses imagination and creativity
- develops confidence and competence
- makes decisions and organises her/his own time and activities
- masters a wide range of skills and concepts
- makes meaning through experiences
- becomes emotionally involved in learning

This latter point reflects Hall's (2005) analysis of neuroscience and its contribution to learning, in which he suggests that 'neuroscience is confirming ... the importance of emotional engagement in learning', which has been accepted since Daniel Goleman first wrote his treatise on emotional development in 1996. What is important about this list is that these are all observable characteristics and, from the perspective of the practitioner, are able to be documented in relation to learning. This is vital insofar as our knowledge and understanding of individual children and their play and learning is concerned. As Papatheodorou suggests: '... children's level of involvement and engagement in play are important indicators of their current development and predictors of their potential.' (p.263). Goouch (2010) is clear about the adults' roles:

> To accompany children in their play is a sophisticated role that can be achieved only by those who know and understand children, who are able to allow the sometimes complex intentions of children at play to take precedence and who will demonstrate respect for such intentionality. (p.55/56).

A demanding task indeed!

Play is not – and should never be – a polarised argument about play versus work ('You can go and play once you've finished your work'). Children work at their play all the time and all 'work' for children should be playful in its approach; that is, child-initiated and child-inspired. This is precisely the strength of approaches such as that adopted by the Reggio Emilia pre-schools, so much admired by many practitioners elsewhere in the world (Smidt, 2012). Play is rarely spoken or written about in relation to Reggio Emilia practices: because it permeates, pervades and is embedded in everything that children and practitioners do everyday there is no need for specificity or a particular focus on play. (I would argue that the reason our focus has now shifted on to play within the early years curriculum in England is because play is still a relatively 'new' concept to policy-makers here.) What we must be aiming for is depth of thinking in children. As Marton and Booth (1997) assert, 'A deep approach to a learning task is characterised by the learner's intention to find meaning in the context through tackling the task ... whereas in a surface approach, focus is rather on meeting the demands of the task as such'.

So there are plenty of arguments, supported by empirical experience in favour of play as a basis, really the basis, for children's learning. Let us now consider what is meant by 'child-initiated' learning experiences.

'Child-initiated' is yet another relatively new term. Previously we often referred to 'child-oriented' experiences but, as readers will see, there is a more than subtle difference here. (I must add that I also prefer the word 'experiences' rather than 'activities', because the latter smacks of just doing something without any necessary benefit, rather than undertaking something which results in learning.) In child-initiated situations the child is at the heart of decision-making: the experiences are often child-inspired, child-directed, child-led, child-managed and child rich! In such situations it is the children's voices that are heard, at least in parallel and often equally with practitioners – again, a strength of the Reggio Emilia approach. As Papatheodorou (2006) asserts, 'The individual is valued and supported through collective endeavours and effort ... In this way a child's self-awareness, self-worth and self-esteem derive from how others relate with him/her and the acknowledgement of their contribution to group efforts and work'.

Children's own initiatives must be used and developed because it is only from this basis that practitioners will begin to understand where children are coming from, what experiences, knowledge and skills they already have and how these can be built upon to deal appropriately with the 'unique child' who is such a part of the new EYFS. We must remember that this unique child is made up of many parts: social, emotional, intellectual and physical. This 'whole child', as the large American study 'Eager to Learn' (Bowman et al. 2000) found has 'prodigious enthusiasm and competence for learning'. The report goes on to state that the adults' role is vital in understanding children's metacognitive development and the need for developing higher-order thinking skills. (The importance of encouraging these skills in young children is also recognised in the 'sustained shared thinking' advocated by the EYFS.)

Child-initiated experiences rely on the child being competent and knowledgeable about their own needs and choices. They enable children to work with confidence, persevering for long periods of time and working at levels far higher than those sometimes identified in the planned curriculum. Child-initiated experiences allow children increased ownership and responsibility. A study in Slovakia of pretend play in pre-school children (Gmitrova and Gmitrov 2003) found that, in child-initiated role-play episodes:

- significantly more cognitive behaviours associated with thinking, knowing and remembering emerged
- children's persistence and thinking behaviours increased
- children took greater pleasure in play and learning

The authors concluded that child-initiated play effectively supports children's problem-solving skills, social skills, literacy and mathematics.

The 1999 High/Scope Report is equally clear that child-initiated learning experiences (rather than what it calls 'scripted academic instruction') foster social responsibility and skills in children 'so that they less often need treatment for emotional impairment or disturbance and are less arrested for felonies as young adults' (ECCD Briefs p.3). A couple of years earlier, in 1997, the High/Scope Foundation also reported that in child-initiated experiences children were more interpersonally interactive and had a greater variety of negotiation strategies. They also showed 'the greatest mastery of basic reading, language and mathematics skills' (Schweinhart 1997).

In David Whitebread's independence project (2007), he and his team found that self-regulated learning – the near equivalent of child-initiated learning in which young children are able to take control of and be responsible for their own learning – significantly benefited children's motivation and progess. Whitebread emphasises that we must see education as something we do with children rather than to them. Darling (1994) asserts that:

> Once children see education as something that other people do to them ... they lose the ability to take any initiative or responsibility for their own learning ... we could and should have classrooms where learning is largely self-motivated.

The best early years practices will be able to accomplish this.

That the new EYFS (DfE 2012) makes such little mention of child-initiated activities is unwelcome: there is some information in the *Early Years Foundation Stage Profile* document (DfE, 2013) which states:

Child-initiated

> The action of a child choosing to extend, repeat or explore an activity. This activity may or may not have been introduced or prompted by an adult. It is the child's innovation within or of the activity which is important and relevant to child initiation. An adult may be present and may be supportive but not directive ... Child initiated activity and exploration provides an important insight into the depth of a child's learning. (p.48)

Earlier in the document it asserts:

> Where learning is secure it is likely that children often initiate the use of

that learning. Judgements about this are made through observing behaviour that a child demonstrates consistently and independently, in a range of situations. Attainment in this context will assure practitioners of the child's confidence and ownership of the specific knowledge, skill or concept being assessed. (p.10)

Play and child-initiated learning – the role of practitioners

We now turn to the huge role for practitioners in child-initiated learning. Play is firmly situated within a framework related to the overall developmental needs of young children (Sutton-Smith 2005), although it's fair to say that there is, as yet, no definitive research to show the value or importance of play for young children or its efficacy as a medium for learning (BERA SIG 2003; Smith 2005).

Child-initiated learning can be situated within other important modern learning theories; for example:

- the well-known Vygotskian concept of scaffolding (learning through the support of a knowledgeable other)
- assisted performance (Tharp and Gallimore 1989) (learning through modelling and the provision of structure by adults or children)
- dialogic enquiry (Wells 1999) (co-construction of knowledge by adults or other children engaging in joint activity together, mediated through language)
- guided participation (Rogoff *et al.* 2001) (context-based joint learning experiences between adults and children using guided observation)
- relational pedagogy (Papatheodorou and Moyles 2008) (learning taking place through the development of both social and cognitive relationships)

All of these emphasise the role of the adult in supporting – rather than directing – the child's developing knowledge and understanding in differing ways. The 'transmission mode' of teaching, sometimes called 'direct teaching', has no place in any of these theories. Neither has the 'old' play method, whereby children were very much left to their own devices once the practitioner had provided play activities for the session (Moyles and Adams 2001). There is significant evidence, as we shall see, that child-initiated learning appears to enable children to play with confidence, persevering for longer periods of time and working at levels far higher than those sometimes identified in a planned curriculum.

There are many skills required of practitioners if they are to be effective in developing child-initiated play practices. It is clear that what is needed is a very special kind of practitioner who can be extremely playful and flexible, but who also has specific knowledge and excellent communication skills. A practitioner who thoroughly understands child development and early years curricula in general and, in particular, each unique child who comes under her/his responsibility in the setting (Moyles *et al.* 2002). In Reggio Emilia preschools practitioners see themselves as 'guides who are learning with the children and adopt a listening role that seeks to encourage thinking, negotiation and the exploration of difference' (The Scottish Government 2006). Following a visit to Reggio Emilia, Papatheodorou (2006) reports:

> *Pedagogistas, atelieristas and other preschool staff carefully plan and explore, in advance, the possible directions that proposed projects may take and the resources required ... [adults] work out the complexity of proposed projects and the systematic and gradual facilitation and scaffolding required in order to assist children ... it removes the potential danger and pitfalls of direct instruction.*
>
> *... as the project develops and many proposals are made by the children, the preschool staff have to make a judgement which they will follow through. This is where children's engagement and motivation become the key criteria. By going through the process of careful planning, the adults know well what they expect the children to achieve; the children have to find this out for themselves through the facilitation of the adults.*

According to Katz and Chard (2000), this kind of curriculum experience allows the child to become an expert, which both empowers the child and allows appropriate dispositions to learning to evolve.

Whitebread's research project (2007: 231), offers a range of general pedagogical points and insights of which the following list is a small selection.

- children learnt a great deal by watching one another
- given the opportunity to make their own choices and decisions, the children were remarkably focused and organized and pursued their own plans and agendas with persistence and sometimes over long periods of time
- sometimes, when an adult became involved in an activity, the children were more inclined to say they couldn't do something, but if they were working with another child they were less likely to question their ability and often mimicked the other child, gaining confidence in their abilities

- the most effective response the practitioner gave to a child asking for help was to refer them to another child who has greater competence or expertise in the particular area
- sometimes it is best for adults not to intervene in children's disputes and disagreements in collaborative play, but to give them time and space to resolve issues themselves
- there is an important distinction between praise (which produces 'adult-pleasers') and encouragement (which gives information, feedback and supports independence).

Can we identify specific practitioner skills which follow from the above? Those identified in a range of research projects and theoretical and practical papers, include:

- careful observation by practitioners of children's play so that they know when (and when NOT) to intervene
- observation (and modelling) of, and by, adults and other children
- adults (and other children) modelling appropriate language and values in their everyday experiences
- listening – adults must recognise that children are worth listening to and show that they value and respect children's oral contributions in a genuine two-way dialogue
- not asking questions – adults can learn much about children by engaging in a mutually respectful dialogue, rather than in asking endless questions
- resourcing the environment – a key factor in ensuring that children are able to initiate their own activities is having an environment where there is a predictable arrangement of resources so that children can readily and easily access materials when they decide to do so

In curriculum planning, space must be left for children's own experiences to have a major place. In Reggio Emilia, for example, the practitioners themselves work through a topic or focus prior to engaging the children in it, to ensure that they can predict the ways children might choose to experience the curriculum:

- experiences provided for the children must be stimulating (accomplished by adults understanding children's interests and needs) and achievable (accomplished by adults understanding each child's present state of development)
- encouraging socio-dramatic/role play – this kind of play is known particularly

to encourage independent and creative thinking (see Broadhead 2004 and 2007) and to allow children choices and autonomy

- encouraging, praising and interacting in a way that encourages sustained, shared thinking without making the children feel that they are subservient to the adults' views and needs
- co-construction of meaning – we have to recognise as adults that we don't always know more than the children, especially when it comes to play! We have to make efforts to understand their thinking in order to tune into their meanings and stand a chance of truly participative dialogue for both adults and children
- respecting children and their choices – children will always respond in ways that are different from adults, but adults need to recognise that this does not make a child's response inferior: just different!
- viewing and treating children as competent learners rather than as immature adults
- recognising that learning is shaped by context and ethos – if we create an ethos where children are dependent on adults, they will, in turn, respond with dependency. Conversely, if we show that we trust and value their judgements, they will endeavour to meet those expectations
- acknowledging children as active agents not passive recipients – children make their own meanings from play and learning situations. We can support extended learning through our recognition that they are active seekers of meaning
- reciprocal interactions – all our interactions with children should show that we value their expertise and can experience life and learning as they see and experience it
- creative and flexible thinking – having a view in one's head that there is only one way learning will happen will not support children. They are flexible and creative thinkers and we must mirror this approach if we are fully to engage with their learning
- 'quiet proximity' – Nind (2001) suggests from her research that we need to operate in 'quiet proximity' to children in order to absorb fully how and what they are learning and, therefore, to know how to interpret and guide their thinking and experiences
- help children rehearse what effective dialogue and communication involves, i.e. thinking, listening and truly sharing experiences without one partner dominating the proceedings (Nind 2001)

- acknowledging self as an equal learner in the adult/child relationship
- analysing one's own practice in depth to understand and assess how one relates to children in play and self-initiated learning experiences

Clearly, there are some big issues here for the training of early years practitioners. In fact, the success or otherwise of operating within an ethos of play and child-initiated learning will depend upon a training programme that enables practitioners to engage thoroughly with issues such as those above.

Discussion

Whilst in principle the EYFS appears to commend this relational pedagogy by which adults and children learn together, there are distinct anomalies which require some thought. One key tenet of the EYFS is the need for practitioners to 'deliver' the curriculum through 'planned and purposeful play' ('Statutory Guidance', para 2.5). This leads me to question how play can be 'planned' if it is to be child-initiated? If learning experiences are truly initiated by the children, planning can only be done in the sense of planning to follow-on from children's expressed interests – and then that depends on the age of the children and the practitioner's knowledge of those children. And what about the word 'purposeful'? To the child, play is always purposeful in that it serves their developmental processes very well. To adults, doing something for a purpose often means activities that work towards the early learning goals. By nature, as we have seen, play is flexible and spontaneous, which makes planning for it highly problematic. Yet we can readily see children learning through play by careful observation and dialogue. Somehow, the language of 'planned and purposeful' smacks of cheating children of their own intentions and purposes, and practitioners will need to be highly aware of this. It would seem that children must play to adult direction which, in itself, cannot be achieved given what has been written about play above.

In addition, the establishment of pre-set learning goals clearly '… hampers practitioners' ability to adopt a play approach because many will not feel confident that this can be done and others interpret such prescription as meaning they must teach children using formal methods in order to achieve goals…' (CD-ROM, *Effective Practice: Play and Exploration*, DfES 2007).

There is subtle and disturbing wording, too, in the repeated EYFS statement 'play-based activities' (not straightforwardly 'play activities'), which makes one think again of policy-makers assuming that practitioners can subvert or bend children's play to their own ends. A key principle of play and child-initiated learning is that it is based wholly on the child's choice and wholly on decisions made by the child.

I have said elsewhere (Moyles 2005) that no-one would deny that play in educational settings should have learning consequences. This is what separates play in that context from recreational play. Practitioners need to be able to show quite clearly that, and what, children are learning through play. However, this does not mean that practitioners must engage in direct instruction techniques in order to achieve these ends. Rather, as the evidence above shows, it is eminently possible, through child-initiated experiences, carefully and sensitively planned, provided for and supported by adults, for children's play to become their chief means of learning in their earliest years (Moyles, 2012). Indeed, this is exactly how the research evidence to date suggests it should be.

Bibliography and references

British Educational Research Association: Early Years Special Interest Group (BERA SIG) (2003), *Early Years Research: Pedagogy, Curriculum and Adult Roles, Training and Professionalism*. Southwell: BERA.

Bowman, B., Donovan, S. and Burns, M. (eds) (2000), *Eager to Learn: Educating our Preschoolers*. Washington, DC: National Academies Press.

Broadhead, P. (2004), Broadhead, P., Howard, J. and Wood, E. (eds) (2010), London: Sage. London: RoutledgeFalmer.

—(2007), *Working Together to Support Playful Learning and Transition*. In J. Moyles (ed.) *Early Years Foundations: Meeting the Challenge*. Maidenhead: Open University Press.

Broadhead, P., Howard, J. and Wood, E. (eds) (2010), *Play and Learning in the Early Years: From Research to Practice*. London: Sage.

Darling, J. (1994), *Child-centred Education and Its Critics*. London: Paul Chapman.

Department for Education (DfE) (2012) *Statutory Framework for the Early Years Foundation Stage*. London: DfE.

DfE (2013), London: Standards and Testing Agency. Available online at: www.education.gov.uk/assessment (accessed 5th January, 2013).

Early Childhood Counts (ECCD) (1999), *Preschool child-initiated Learning Found to Help Prevent Later Problems*. Washington, DC: World Bank.

Gmitrova, V. and Gmitrov, G. (2003), 'The Impact of teacher-directed and child-directed pretend play on cognitive competence in kindergarten children'. *Early Childhood Education Journal*. 30(4): 241–6.

Greenfield, S. (2002), 'Face-to-Face' Susan Greenfield. *Interplay*. Questions Publishers. pp.20–3: Summer.

Goleman, D. (1996), *Emotional Intelligence: Why it can matter more than IQ*. London: Bloomsbury Publishing.

Hall, J. (2005), *Neuroscience and Education: A review of the contribution of brain science to teaching and learning*. Glasgow: SCRE Research Report No: 121.

Katz, L. and Chard, S. (2000), *Engaging Children's Minds: The Project Approach* (2edn.). Norwood, NJ: Ablex Publishing.

Kwon Y-I. (2003), *A Comparative Analysis of Preschool Education in Korea and England. Comparative Education*, 39(4): 479–91.

Marton, F. and Booth, S. (1997), *Learning and Awareness*. Mahwah, NJ. Lawrence Erlbaum Associates.

Moyles, J. (2006), *Is Everybody Ready? In Getting Ready for Phonics – L is for sheep*. Featherstone, Bloomsbury Publishing plc.

—(2005), 'Introduction'. In J. Moyles (ed.) *The Excellence of Play* (2edn.) Maidenhead: Open University Press.

—(2012), *A-Z of Play in Early Childhood*. Maidenhead: Open University Press/McGraw Hill.

—(ed) (2010), *Thinking About Play: Developing a Reflective Approach*. Maidenhead: Open University Press/McGraw Hill.

Moyles, J., Adams, S. and Musgrove, A. (2002), *SPEEL: Study of Pedagogical Effectiveness in Early Learning*. London: DfES Research Report 363.

Moyles, J. and Adams, S. (2001), *StEPs: Statements of Entitlement to Play*. Buckingham: Open University Press.

Nind, M. (2001), 'Enhancing the communication learning environment of an early years unit'. Paper presented at the British Educational Research Association Annual Conference, Leeds, September.

Papatheodorou, T. and Moyles, J. (2008, in press) Learning Together in the Early Years: Exploring Relational Pedagogy. London: Routledge.

Papatheodorou, T. (2006), *Seeing the Wider Picture: Reflections on the Reggio Emilia Approach*. Available online at: http://www.tactyc.org.uk/pdfs/Reflection_Papatheodorou.pdf

—(2010), Play and the achievement of potential. In J. Moyles (ed.) *The Excellence of Play* (3ᵉ). Maidenhead: Open University Press/McGraw Hill.

Parliamentary Office of Science and Technology (2000), *Early Years Learning*. London: House of Commons Education and Employment Select Committee.

Pugmire-Stoy, M. (1991), *Spontaneous Play in Early Childhood*. Clifton Park, NY: Delmar Associates.

Rogoff, B. (1998), 'Cognition as a Collaborative Process.' In D. Kohn and R.S. Siegler (eds) *Handbook of Child Psychology*, Vol.2 *Cognition, Perception and Language* (5edn.). New York: John Wiley.

Rogoff, B., Goodman Turkanis, C. and Bartlett, L. (eds.) (2001), *Learning together: Children and adults in a school community*. New York: Oxford University Press.

Schweinhart, L. (1997), 'child-initiated learning activities for young children living in poverty.' CEEP Archive of ERIC/EECE Digests. Available online at http://ceep.crc.uiuc.edu/eecearchive/digests/1997/schwei97.html

Sheridan, M., Howard, J. and Alderson, D. (2010), *Play in Early Childhood: From Birth to Six Years*. London: Routledge.

Smidt, S. (2012), *Introducing Malaguzzi: Exploring the life and work of Reggio Emilia's founding father*. London: Routledge.

Smith, P. K. (2005), 'Play: Types and Functions in Human Development'. In B. Ellis and D. Bjorklund (eds) *Origins of the Social Mind: Evolutionary Psychology and Child Development*. New York: Guilford Press.

Sutton-Smith, B. (2005), *Play: An Interdisciplinary Synthesis*. Lanham, MD: University Press of America

Sylva, K., Melhuish, E., Sammons, P., Siraj-Blatchford, I., Taggart, B. and Elliot, K. (2003), The Effective Provision of Pre-School Education (EPPE) 'Project: Findings from the Pre-school Period'. London: Institute of Education.

Tharp, R. and Gallimore, R. (1989), *Rousing Minds to Life: Teaching, Learning, and Schooling in Social Context*. Cambridge: University of Cambridge Press.

Vygotsky, L. (1978), *Mind in Society: The development of higher psychological processes*. Cambridge, MA: Harvard University Press.

Vygotsky, L. (1976), 'Play and its role in the mental development of the child'. In. J. Bruner, A. Jolly and K. Sylva (eds) *Play: its role in development and evolution*. Glasgow: Penguin.

Wells, G. (1999), *Dialogic Inquiry: Towards a Socio-cultural Practice and Theory of Education*. Cambridge: University of Cambridge Press.

Whitebread, D. (2007), 'Developing Independence in Learning'. In J. Moyles (ed.) *Early Years Foundations: Meeting the Challenge*. Maidenhead: Open University Press.

Whitebread, D. (2010), *Developmental Psychology and Early Childhood Education: A Guide for Students and Practitioners*. London: Sage.

Wyse, D. and Goswami, U. (2008), 'Synthetic phonics and the teaching of reading'. *British Educational Research Journal* 34(6), 691-710.

Part 2: Curriculum and environment

Ros Bayley and Lynn Broadbent: Child-initiated learning and developing children's talk 4

This is a true story.

Ravi wasn't known for being talkative. In fact, it would be more accurate to say that his reticence to engage in any form of conversation with either children or adults was causing considerable concern. He often seemed to be 'far away,' and was very quiet during focused activities, speaking only when he was spoken to. Throughout child-initiated learning sessions he would spend long periods of time watching other children but saying nothing, and it was rare for him to spend more than a few minutes on any activity. It seemed he had nothing that he was willing to communicate, to adults or children.

All efforts by staff to engage him seemed doomed to failure until when, at the end of one lunchtime, his key worker returned hot, flustered and almost late from a trip to the local market. She carried with her a large plastic bag that the children found very intriguing. They implored her to let them see what was inside. Obligingly she opened the bag to reveal the Spiderman figure she had bought for her son's birthday. It was then that the most surprising thing happened. Ravi leapt to his feet, and grasping the figure, proceeded to give the assembled company a blow-by-blow account of the life history of Spiderman. In the next five minutes he spoke more than he had in the entire time he had been attending the setting. He was animated, excited and brimming over with enthusiasm. In those significant minutes Ravi demonstrated something simple and obvious, but frequently forgotten: that each and every one of us talks with most interest and enthusiasm when we are speaking about the things that are important to us!

And that is precisely why child-initiated learning offers such a wonderful context for supporting, developing and extending talk. When children take on the responsibility for organising their own learning they will engage with things that interest them. They are then far more likely to need and to want to talk, and their interests provide them with the stimulus to do that. So if we can find out about the things that are interesting them and then provide access to those things in a culture of encouragement and support, talk will flourish!

The physical environment

If curiosity, wonder and puzzlement are fundamental to stimulating children to talk, it follows that they must have access to a wide range of opportunities for imaginative play, both indoors and outside. What are the implications of this for the resources we provide, the sorts of spaces we make available and the ways in which we organise them?

Let's begin by thinking about the spaces. Obviously, what can be done will be governed largely by the constraints imposed by the building and its location. Practitioners are fortunate indeed if they have access to attractive, spacious and safe accommodation for outdoor and indoor play. However, there is a great deal that can be done in even the most unpromising conditions, given imagination, a little thought and a few simple resources.

The first question to ask is, do the spaces in your setting encourage children to talk and interact? Think about the placement of the furniture and other equipment, and the way this affects movement and grouping. While it's right that there should be places for children to be alone, the positioning of chairs, tables, shelving, screens and equipment can all create barriers which will restrict flow and inhibit those priceless opportunities for a child to suddenly come across what another is doing and become interested by it.

We are not advocating one large open space with no demarcation. It's helpful to have some areas dedicated to particular uses, for example special places where children can display their pictures, drawings, models and other things that are important to them. You might want to designate a storytelling corner or set up a storyteller's chair where children can go to retell stories, and to arrange an attractive reading corner with a wide range of texts, including magazines, catalogues, comics and maps. If you have the space and the equipment you will find that a performance area with microphones, musical instruments and players will be very popular and will encourage children to talk.

There needs to be a separation of quiet and noisy activities, both inside and out. Thoughtful planning can help achieve a balance. Why not encourage children to share responsibility for the way the physical space is used by getting them involved in decisions about how the working areas will be organised? This in itself will generate talk.

Next, think about what goes into the spaces you have created. Are there plenty of objects and artefacts that will capture children's interest and motivate discussion? Some of these will be bought, others may be borrowed, begged or just found. For example, simple digital cameras are a fantastic resource, enabling children to photograph their projects, keep a record of the things that are important to them, and return to these later to talk about them. A range of open-ended materials – such as cardboard boxes, blankets and drapes, telephones, walkie-talkies, masks, dressing-up clothes – will stimulate imaginative play. Puppets and dolls (home-made as well as commercially produced) have no end of uses for developing thinking and conversation. Model yourself the ways in which they can be used, and involve the children in making their own puppets and props to support role play and imaginative play.

It has been said many times that although child-initiated learning cannot be planned, it is vital that it is planned for. So how can we plan for child-initiated learning to encourage talk?

One of the times when people talk is when they are sharing experiences and ideas; therefore it is important to select resources and activities that maximise sharing behaviours. There are certain materials that by their nature bring children together for play and conversation; for example, heavy things like logs, boxes and boards that need several children to move them, and large items such as wheel-barrows and buckets that can be filled and emptied. Another time when people talk is when they have a problem or are in conflict. Do you support children in solving their own conflicts and resolving their own difficulties, teaching and modelling the relevant vocabulary? Do you have high expectations for the way children communicate, introducing them to new and exciting vocabulary?

The last and most important element of the environment is the people in it. Children will take a lead from the behaviour of the adults they see. Ask yourself, do the adults in your setting display a variety of roles for children? Do children see adults taking messages, modelling greetings and demonstrating other uses of transactional language, speaking and listening to each other? Adults should involve themselves in children's play in ways that enable them to give children active examples of the use of language. And if you want children to model their behaviour on what you do you will need to give them access to some of the things you use. Do you make resources used in adult-initiated activities available for children to use during periods of child-initiated learning?

The daily routine

Arranging the physical space so that it is a place where talk will flourish is one thing, but we must also pay close attention to the structure of the daily routine to ensure that children have sufficient time to become engrossed in the things that they want to talk about. Adults must be on hand to engage in meaningful conversations and 'scaffold' and support children's talk. If all the available adults are involved in focused activities many potentially rich opportunities for promoting talk will be lost! Encourage children to talk with one another throughout the daily routine in order to share experiences and gather new information. If a child asks a question, refer it to other children for them to suggest and share answers. If a child has a particular skill (anything from whistling, to counting backwards, to drawing) arrange opportunities for them to teach it to others.

Quality interaction

Any setting committed to promoting quality talk during periods of child-initiated learning needs practitioners who are prepared to strive to develop their skills of interaction. It is only when the supporting adults themselves have these skills that children will gain maximum benefit from the experiences offered. Children need access to adults who really value what they have to say about their self-initiated learning, and who make time to listen to them. So encourage children to express their thoughts and feelings, and support them in talking about their ideas and in describing and reflecting on their actions. Plan activities that enable children to repeat, consolidate and practise language.

Some of the children in your setting may not be from English speaking backgrounds. Value children's community languages, and try to provide opportunities for them sometimes to be spoken within the setting. Getting a child to teach others how to say simple words (for example greetings, thanks or the names of days) in a language different from the one normally spoken in the setting not only openly values that language, but also encourages children to think and talk about what language does and how it is used. Bilingual support practitioners can be enormously helpful here. (Editor's note: For further discussion of bilingualism in child-initiated activities see the chapter by Theodora Papatheodorou which starts on page 112.)

It is also likely that you will encounter children who are experiencing particular problems in communicating through talk. Perhaps they are having difficulties with their language development, or maybe with their speech or hearing. It is important for practitioners to respond sensitively to any particular issues they know about or become aware of. This not only requires special attention to the needs of the child in the setting, but also means involving parents and working closely with specialist services.

When you know what works you can do more of it on purpose!

As a practitioner or parent it is salutary to remember that children can and do learn without adults. They learn, we hope, from the materials and experiences we provide and what we say to them; but in the early years they probably learn even more from each other, and they work things out for themselves. Nevertheless, when a talented adult skilfully enters a play scenario children's learning and talk can accelerate dramatically. And if the entry is not skilful (or the adult not talented!) the opposite can be true. Here is a true anecdote which describes the experience of one of the writers. To spare her blushes, and to avoid giving the reader any clue as to which of us it might be, let's call her Roxanne!

Roxanne was a young teacher fresh from her first experience of teaching. She had begun in Key Stage 2, but the following year she was moved to the reception class. She was very indignant about this. Wasn't it going backwards? Weren't the older children more important, and therefore teaching them carried more prestige? She didn't think she'd done that badly in Key Stage 2! Nevertheless she set to, and much to her surprise found herself enjoying it.

One day a large group of children were playing happily in the home corner. Armed with the arrogance of ignorance, Roxanne set out to make sure that they were, as she saw it, doing something profitable and learning effectively. Her intention was to scaffold their talk and extend their vocabulary. While she began firing questions at them they, imperceptibly at first, began to remove pieces of the play furniture they were using to another part of the room. Roxanne was far too busy asking questions to be aware of what was happening, until it dawned on her that the children had moved the entire piece of play away to another area and she was on her own! It then, suddenly occurred to her that the children may not actually want her involvement! They had been too polite to tell her to go away and had solved the problem by going somewhere else, where Roxanne wasn't.

That day provided a valuable lesson. If play is to be truly child-initiated then it must be owned by the players. In other words, we adults need to be invited in. We need to know how to interact in ways that give children options, to participate and not direct, and we need to be clear about the various roles we can play.

High/Scope offers a useful framework for classifying adult/child interaction. There are three different roles the adult can adopt:

1 The manager (this is the person who completely ignores the children's agenda

and attempts to impose her own. She interferes with the children's play and when she does this rich and profitable talk is not going to happen!)

2   The observer (this is the person who, as long as the children are playing nicely and not bothering her, is quite content to let them get on with things while she does something that she regards as more important)

3   The co-player (this describes the person who is able to enter the children's play sensitively and unobtrusively in order to develop their talk and their learning)

It is obvious that, out of these three, we are likely to have the greatest impact by taking on the role of the co-player. In order to do this we need to pay careful attention to the process by which we become involved in what the children are doing.

Initially take time to observe and understand what is happening within the play. Listen carefully to what the children have to say and note the way in which they are using materials. When you have tuned into their process you are then in a position to choose to enter the play, or not. You may at this point decide that to become involved would be destructive and that your presence would only be an intrusion. If this is the case, the sensible action is to 'creep away' and allow the children to continue on their own, or to make a conscious decision to take on the role of the observer and watch inconspicuously from a discreet distance. Or you may decide that there are opportunities and benefits from becoming a co-player.

In order to enter into the play sensitively and unobtrusively it is important to begin by establishing a comfortable rapport with the children. Take things stage by stage and try not to rush the process. Join the children at their physical level. If we are to become play partners it is essential that we do our best to 'shrink' to the same size as the children, which invariably results in us spending periods of time kneeling, squatting and even lying on the floor! Then simply start to play alongside. Unless children actively engage you in conversation, stay quiet for a while.

Pick up some of the animals, figures, whatever the children aren't using and begin your own game. Use the materials yourself, modelling what the children are doing. Engage in 'self-talk,' describing quietly what you are doing and labelling your actions as you carry them out. Once the children are comfortable with your presence, begin to initiate parallel talk. Be alert for natural opportunities for conversation. When children are deeply involved in doing something they don't always want to talk about it, and it is important to respect this. Wait for occasions when they interrupt their play and pause to reflect. Not only is such a situation more conducive to talk, it may also help the child to clarify 'where next'. Used well, this process will generally lead you to a place where you will be invited to join the play. You are now in the position of co-player, able to extend both the language and the learning. It is a privileged position. Enjoy it, and respect it.

Finally, involve yourself in the play. Be excited about what is happening. Discuss the children's ideas and look for opportunities to extend their thinking. At this point you might make suggestions for how the play could proceed, being prepared, of course, for the children to reject your suggestions (it is, after all, their game). Ask questions sparingly, and when you do ask them make them open-ended, and questions to which you genuinely want to know the answer rather than phatic 'questions for the sake of questioning'. Relate your questions directly to what the child is doing and ask them about their thought process. Add materials that move the play on and build on the children's ideas. Continue to observe and listen carefully, taking your lead from the children. When engaged in activities of their own choosing, children generally have a very clear sense of purpose and will become deeply engaged in what they are doing. It is when adults tune into this process that the most productive conversations ensue. Attempts to introduce another agenda usually result in lost opportunities and frustration for the child.

Supporting children with language delay

Almost all children talk to themselves as they play, giving a running commentary on their actions. Vygotsky has shown how essential this is to the development of thinking. He refers to such talk as an 'exterior monologue', which in turn develops into an 'internal monologue', which then becomes thought. However, for children who may have come from language impoverished backgrounds such talk may be scanty and vague, restricting their cognitive development. This is when talk during child-initiated learning can make a dramatic difference. With the right support children can absorb new vocabulary and language structures easily, because the talk can be directly linked to the things that they are doing, making it real, meaningful and easily understood.

... so here are a few important things to do:

- Use the children's comments as conversation openers. Listen attentively to what they are saying, repeating their words back to them. This affirms what they are saying and builds their confidence
- Ask questions sparingly. Too much questioning can distract children's attention from the things that are important to them. It can also undermine

their confidence by 'putting them on the spot'. A question can be very intimidating if the child lacks the language with which to answer. When you do ask a question don't demand an immediate response. Allow plenty of time for the child to reply

- Respect the children's ideas. Be curious about how they are doing things, and let them know you are interested
- Expand and extend what they are doing by introducing new ideas and vocabulary into the conversation. However, take care not to overwhelm the child. Give him or her a model that is achievable. Remodel (rather than correct) inaccuracies
- Give plenty of visual support. Wherever possible, illustrate what you are saying with pictures, photographs and artefacts
- Describe your own actions when you work alongside the child. When observing, sometimes model the use of an 'exterior monologue' by describing the child's actions as they occur: for example, I see you are making a garage for the trucks ... and you've used all the large bricks ... . This helps children acquire a relevant vocabulary. But be patient and leave plenty of gaps in your commentary to enable the child to contribute or take over the lead
- Plan further activities and experiences that enable the child to repeat and consolidate the language they have learned. Remember that child-initiated learning is an extremely potent vehicle for the development of spoken language!

'It is easy to inhibit children's learning through our own desire to teach.'

We are not at all sure who first said this, but it is a very profound statement. Certainly young Roxanne, with the best of intentions, ran the risk of doing just that. In a culture of education driven by targets the perceived need to 'teach' and the pressure to deliver all the children to the next stage at a prescribed level (regardless of the time of the year they were born!) can all too easily dominate. Adults can become obsessed with achievement criteria, worried if they are unable to tick all the boxes. We beg you not to forget that children can – and do – learn language effortlessly and abundantly when it is linked to something important to them and within their experience.

Wendy Scott: Child-initiated writing

5

Speaking and writing both provide ways of conveying messages; they are also both means of developing and refining ideas. The key feature of writing is its permanence. Something written down can be referred to later, at a different time and in a different context. For this reason it has been said that writing is the foundation of civilisation for most of the world's cultures. Those few societies that have never evolved a written script have not developed in the same ways, or to the same extent, as those that have. Learning to write is one of the most important skills for children to acquire.

Writing involves compositional skills in deciding what to write, drawing on imagination as well as experience, and developing a sense of narrative together with a sense of style. It also requires necessary secretarial skills of handwriting and spelling. The complexities of learning to write are not always recognised by adults who have mastered these skills, but do not recall the long processes involved in their learning (even if they appreciate their own continuing development in their first and other languages and scripts). Parents have the privilege of watching the beginnings of the communicative process from their child's birth, and can see how differently children in the same family develop from the start. This chapter is for them, and for staff working with children from around six months to six or seven years old, in the Early Years Foundation Stage (EYFS) and Key Stage 1. It celebrates the power of children's thinking, underlines the importance of meaning and motivation, and suggests ways in which adults can recognise, encourage, support and extend the development of child-initiated writing. References include the Guidance for the Early Years Foundation Stage and the expectations of the Primary Strategy. The aim is to support the application of principled, professional judgement informed by knowledge of literacy development, allied to insight into the characteristics of individual children as emerging writers.

Writing is a very sophisticated form of symbolic representation, intimately linked to reading; both are grounded in verbal language and the drive to communicate. Vygotsky (1986) showed that the natural function of symbols is to be found first in communication. Because we communicate symbolically, we think and remember symbolically. Speaking, reading and writing enable us to exchange signs that convey shared meanings. Children growing up in a literate society are surrounded by images as well as sounds, and soon start to interpret those that have significance for them.

The power of children's thinking

From birth, babies are dedicated to making sense of their world. Interactions that engage the joint attention of adults and children are often initiated by babies, and are most effective when adults tune in and offer a warm and relevant response. Labelling objects, events and ideas begins in earliest infancy and helps babies to identify words as specific areas of meaning. First words are generally names for things, and demonstrate ways of classifying what the child can see, hear and feel. These words refer to first hand experiences, but can also represent more generalised concepts. Infants' personal associations and particular interests within their home environment are significant influences on their development.

Confident children actively seek new experiences and information, which become increasingly available to them as their independence grows, serving both to modify their understanding and to stimulate further enquiry. Gopnik, Meltzoff and Kuhl (1999) show how children's drive to understand leads them to experiment with, as well as to imitate, events in their surroundings. They learn to talk by being spoken to as conversational partners, and this leads them to apply what they perceive as rules of language to their speech. For example, children commonly generate plurals by adding an 's', applying this rule which they have worked out for themselves to words they have never heard: for instance, mouses or sheeps. Over time, the conventions of speech are internalised.

Young children are natural mimics, and when they see people around them writing, they want to do it too. They want to copy what they observe as adult behaviour and, as their motor skills develop, they want to 'have a go' at shaping letters. When adults and older children respond to their efforts to produce signs and symbols, they begin the dual process of decoding and encoding text as part of their active response to the world around them. Many draw on their knowledge of sounds to invent spelling before they can read fluently. This is an important stage in getting ready for writing, when children are driven to explore and express meaning. What the child has written often looks like squiggles, with an occasional (almost) recognisable letter. The interesting thing is that, although this 'emergent writing' may look like no more than a few random scribblings to us, the child can very often 'read' it back to us, and will if asked. There are dangers in imposing unrealistic standards related to conventional form and function on children who are practising this very early writing, Premature expectations of accurate spelling and presentation can result in counter-productive pressures which will most probably lead to loss of confidence and the rapid evaporation of motivation.

Meaning

The realisation that their own name and other words can be written down, that lists are useful and that notes assist communication, helps young children to understand the significance of writing and stimulates them to try it for themselves. Hall and Robinson (1995) demonstrate how, in their quest for meaning, young children are active agents in their own literacy learning. Making and maintaining explicit links between oracy, reading and writing reinforces and extends their growing interest and understanding. Adults who know a child well can interpret their attempts at pronunciation or decoding print, and also encourage their emergent writing. In her detailed case study of early writing, Bissex (2004) showed that this is effective for purposes which make sense to the child, in the context of real life.

David et al (2000) point out that children decode their own drawings and early writing when they wish to convey messages. A summer-born girl of nearly five who drew expressively but had only ever written her name independently, worked out how to write 'almonds', having eaten and enjoyed some. She was rewarded by the delight of her family, who understood the significance of her effort, and realised that the underlining represented the presentation in her school book.

Children learning another language at home have particular challenges when, unlike English, it is written from right to left. Yazan, in the following example, taken from Kenner (2004), experimented with his name in both orientations. In addition he tried English as well as Arabic script. This gives an indication of the enormous complexity of the demands which he is processing.

The pre-schools in Reggio Emilia work through an emergent curriculum, following up children's own ideas, interpretations, thoughts and theories. The examples show how one six-year-old represented communication through music, another showed a conversational exchange between two people, and a third illustrated the varied timbre of different languages.

A singing voice

Message

Different languages

Motivation

The examples shown illustrate the power of young children's thinking and the strength of their determination to make and share meaning. It is important that this drive is respected and encouraged. On entry to nursery or school children should have opportunities to show what they already know, and to continue to initiate and develop their own ideas. Dweck (2006) makes it clear that praise for effort is more effective than rewarding performance. Adults can do much to encourage children's determination to practise and improve by appreciating their attempts to express themselves. The best approach is to treat writing as a tool or stimulus to thought, rather than allowing its purpose to be simply a way of pleasing adults. Give children free rein to express themselves. Insisting on the correct formation of letters before children have developed the necessary fine motor skills is counter-productive (Wray and Medwell, 2007).

Play which is within the child's control is a great motivator and has a central role in learning. In play, children can explore ideas and take risks. They can try things out and extend the limits of what they know without fear of failure, so they remain free to be creative and flexible. This in turn leads to a sense of mastery, which motivates them to strive for improvement in spite of difficulties and confusions. As summarised by Moyles (2006), English is phonetically less regular than most other languages. Spelling poses considerable challenges, so learners need plenty of time as well as rich experience of speech and reading to foster the development of their writing skills. In the early stages, adults need to learn to interpret children's intentions: one five-year-old whose compositional skills were advanced well beyond his ability to write them down, managed to express his thinking through typing. The meaning of logical but unconventional spellings, for example 'fam' for 'farmer', could be deduced from the context of his complex stories. Use of a keyboard can help to release children's creativity by removing the physical barriers to forming letters, enabling them to get their thoughts down in writing.

A three-year-old, able to express her poetic imagination verbally, was helped to capture her ideas by her mother, who scribed her first poem.

> *The snake hanging from a branch upon a tree*
> *Behind from a branch on a tree he hang on a branch*
> *(It's a snake that's a boy) who was very prickly.*
> *It was very prickly because there was a fire. On board of his back there was a fire*
> *What on the branch of the lisp of the snake he hang on his branch.*
> *He swivelled his words when all of a sudden he sivelled his way of words*
> *And he cockled and he went sliver and he opened his wide mouth when Squeak came past.*
> *And on a lisp he spoke with a hisp, he spoke with a kick upon the hook*
> *And severed his way when all of a sudden semp cockereleaf of mefficork*
> *And clapped its hands and went ha ha ha, hee ha ha because it was a snake.*

And pork of a sudden it saw a badger!
Maybe coming near or close it was a badger set.
And hang a lisp it's a snake that eats the badger down its throat
And swallows and swallows and swallows and swallows down its throat.

There is a wonderful feeling for language here; the made-up words, the repetition and the stream of consciousness leaps in narrative and logic are reminiscent of James Joyce! This three-year-old was clearly fired by and absorbed in the reptilian nature of the snake, and able orally to capture its essence, its snakiness. Her mother appreciated the child's creativity and gave it status by writing her words down. In doing so she also confirmed the importance of writing.

The process of composition is invisible, and wanting to share thoughts with others is a good reason for writing. It is important that, as they try to master secretarial skills, children sustain their desire to express their ideas. This is helped when they have a model and purpose for writing, so their home environment is highly significant, with siblings as well as parents influencing their progress. Children's emerging skills are reinforced when their early attempts at writing are taken seriously.

Conversely, they can be damaged if they are ridiculed or ignored.

Supporting emergent writing

Young children learn from the routines, expectations, and the ethos of their home and nursery setting or school. Where they experience authentic activities and stimulating contexts for literacy, they will initiate much written communication in their own ways. A frequent starting point is with pictures that tell a story, either their own pictures and story, or one they've been told or had read to them. Promoting early writing is much more than teaching shapes and the relationship between sounds and letters. It depends on the concentration and persistent effort that result from deep involvement, and flourishes in curious and confident children who are supported by constructive relationships.

Alexander, a three-year-old who produced the following example, said, 'It's a car … look, steps … now it's a train!' His preoccupation with circles, right angles, vertical lines and zigzag shapes is echoed in the 'writing' emerging above his picture.

The table 'Game scores' is a record of scores in an outdoor game. It shows how three four-year-olds have written their own names and then made a tally of the skittles they have knocked over. It involves early mathematics as well as literacy.

Name	How many bottles?		
D aŋa	|||		
LUCyLyh	ʇʇ	ʇʇ++	
/ ᴍ4	/		

The four-year-old who wrote the invitation to the garden party has produced a comprehensible message for a real purpose: 'Come to the garden party, 21st July', enhanced by the lively illustration.

Stella's shopping list includes cheese, peas, cucumber, lettuce, celery and fish. She was five when she wrote this, and clearly has experience of shopping lists and their use.

All forms of representation, including expressive movement that develops gross as well as fine motor skills, help in the process of refining transcription, which is closely linked to drawing, and to reading too. Socio-dramatic play outside as well as indoors can provide meaningful contexts for writing, reinforced through responsive interactions with adults. Bromley (2006) suggests a rich range of practical strategies to encourage both authorial and secretarial skills in the Foundation Stage and Key Stage 1, which are based on children's interests and initiatives.

Current expectations

Many parents, as well as early years advisers, academics, teachers and practitioners have been concerned by the particular emphasis on formal literacy in the Early Years Foundation Stage (EYFS) in England. In spite of this widespread concern about the level of expectations set for children who may be only just five at the end of the reception year, the revised Early Years Profile (EYP) still demands considerable levels of phonic knowledge. It is worth noting that, in her Review of the EYFS (DfE 2011) Dame Clare Tickell recommended that assessment should be based primarily on the observation of daily activities that illustrate children's embedded learning, and that the EYFS requirement relating to delivery through play is clarified. However, she suggested that the highest level of achievement measured through the EYFS Profile should be aligned to Level 1 in the National Curriculum, and the Early Learning Goal (ELG) for writing states that 'children use their phonic knowledge to write words in ways which match their spoken sounds. They also write some irregular common words. They write simple sentences which can be read by themselves and others. Some words are spelt correctly and others are phonetically plausible'. In practice this means that children are generally introduced to a system of phonics from the age of three or four, and this trend has been reinforced through the introduction in 2012 of a statutory phonics check for all children in Year 1. The pilot for this check the previous year showed that many children were confused by the inclusion of non-words, and that more able readers had particular problems. This is predictable, given the way that early readers rely on context and other cues to make sense of what they are de-coding. Many questions remain about the predictive value of the check, and there are valid concerns about the effects of this decontextualised approach, particularly as the results, analysed by month of birth, show achievement to be significantly related to age. A year in the life of a five or six year old makes a relatively big difference to their experience and maturation, which means that there are dangers in simplistic measurements of achievement, especially as the phonics check results do not correlate with the teacher assessments made a year later at the end of Key Stage 1. Because of the close relationship between reading and writing, this narrow approach has implications for children's achievements across the curriculum; anecdotal evidence suggests that a restricted phonic approach to literacy results in difficulties in spelling later.

In England, there are continuing concerns that the expectations at the end of the EYFS, now compounded by parents' as well as teachers' anxiety around the phonics check in Year 1, tend to push decontextualised phonics training down into nursery settings, as well as distorting teaching in the reception year. Teachers responding to a survey by the United Kingdom Literacy Association in 2012 (UKLA 2012) raised many concerns about the check, which is but one example of the way that high stakes testing affects teaching and learning. It is worth referring to the *Cambridge Review of the Primary Curriculum* (Alexander, 2009) for rigorously researched evidence on purposes and principles as well as content of the curriculum. While affirming the crucial importance of reading and writing for learning, the report includes the recommendation that the pedagogy endorsed for the EYFS should continue at least into Year 1.

In this context, the guidance and explanatory notes for the literacy ELGs published in the *Statutory Guidance to the EYFS Profile* (Standards and Testing Agency, 2012) are welcome, in that they reinforce the importance of a broad approach to early reading and writing, which are mutually reinforcing in practice.

Specifically in relation to writing, Early Learning Goal 10 expects that: 'Children use their phonic knowledge to write words in ways which match their spoken sounds. They also write some irregular common words. They write sentences which can be read by themselves and others. Some words are spelt correctly and others are phonetically plausible.' The statutory guidance makes it clear that: 'The child writes for a range of purposes in meaningful contexts. The child's writing may include features of different forms such as stories, lists, labels, captions, recipes, instructions and letters. The child's writing is phonetically plausible when he or she writes simple regular words and particularly when he or she attempts to write more complex words. The child and others can read and make sense of the text.'

It is important to note that children in Wales, Scotland and Northern Ireland, as well as most other developed countries, are not expected to be able to blend and segment sounds in words in their reading and writing at the level of detail that is expected of children in England at the age of five. Research (Suggate 2013) endorses a later start to formal literacy, showing that children learning to read later catch up with children who start earlier: around the age of ten, children beginning to read at seven had caught up to those having formal lessons at five. Later starters had no long-term disadvantages in decoding and reading fluently, and had better reading comprehension. This research suggests that a focus on early reading and writing could be relaxed in favour of plenty of broader literacy experience, including verbal communication. Indeed, Sykes *et al* (2009) found worryingly high levels of children being wrongly diagnosed as having special needs in the reception year, particularly those who are summer born and boys, who generally mature later than girls.

The literacy ELGs have been controversial since they were introduced, and the results for writing have been consistently lower than averages across other areas of learning. Many childcare and early education experts have argued for some time that the expectations at the end of the Foundation Stage rush children into formal learning too soon. (e.g. House 2011; Palmer 2010; Wyse, 2006; Macrory, 2001). Goswami and Bryant (2007) point to the wide individual differences between children in the early and primary years. They contend that thinking, reasoning and understanding can be enhanced by pretend play, with opportunities to write embedded in the play. They highlight the need for scaffolding by the teacher to help individual children, and they remind us that maps, music and maths have distinctive genres of representation. Work led by Glenda Walsh in Northern Ireland (Sproule et al 2005) suggests that a delay in formal literacy teaching coupled with a focus on emergent skills avoids early misidentification of children as failures and results in greater motivation as well as raised attainment later. A study commissioned by the Department for Children, Schools and Families, (DfE, 2010) compares how children score in the early learning goals with how they perform in literacy and numeracy tests at the end of Key Stage 1. The research indicates that the two literacy goals 'did not seem crucial' to high performance once children arrive at school. Instead it suggests that language, communication and thinking skills are strong predictors of a child's ability to read and write. As well as the confident use of spoken language, children's dispositions, attitudes and social development are important influences that help them to become accomplished writers. This confirms that purposeful, child-initiated writing linked to children's interests is more effective in the early years than working towards a formalised goal that is set unrealistically high.

The way forward

It is not easy for schools to counter the pressures resulting from high stakes testing, so it is encouraging to see favourable comments about emergent writing in an

OFSTED report (2008), which noted that young children would take a post-it note while playing and jot down a question or relevant piece of information, using their own form of mark making. This was judged to be a very positive way for them to contribute to their own learning. A specialist survey on literacy (OFSTED 2012) includes the following two relevant main findings:

- The score for writing remains substantially the weakest of all the assessment areas in the Foundation Stage Profile. Girls achieved more highly than boys in all four areas but the gap was widest in writing, where 77% of girls achieved a secure level of performance, but only 58% of boys
- The quality of pupils' learning was hampered in weaker lessons by a number of 'myths' about what makes a good lesson. The factors that most commonly limited learning included: an excessive pace; an overloading of activities; inflexible planning; and limited time for pupils to work independently. Learning was also constrained in schools where teachers concentrated too much or too early on a narrow range of test or examination skills

There is thus support for practitioners who, sharing knowledge with parents and carers, develop their awareness of individual children's previous experience, abilities and needs in the context of their particular interests. They can then combine this with informed knowledge of pedagogy as well as subject expertise. Each one of these aspects confirms the powerful contribution that child-initiated writing makes to literacy, which should be fostered and celebrated as an important stage in learning to write. As the five-year-old son of Glenda Bissex announced on a note pinned to his bedroom door, it is a case of 'GYNYS AT WYRK.'

Bibliography and references

Alexander, R. *et al* (2009), *Children, their World, their Education: final report and recommendations of the Cambridge Primary Review* Routledge Also available online at www.primaryreview.org.uk/

Bissex, G. (2004), reprint edition *Gnys at Wyrk: a child learns to write and read*. Cambridge MA: Harvard University Press.

Bredekamp, S. and Copple, C. (1997) Developmentally Appropriate Practice in Early Childhood Programs. Washington, DC: National Association for the Education of Young Children.

Bromley, H. (2006), *Making My Own Mark*. London: The British Association for Early Childhood Education (BAECE)

Curtis, P (2008), *Early-years writing lessons 'do no good'* http://www.guardian.co.uk/education/2008/jul/14/schools.uk

DfES (2007), Statutory Framework and Practice Guidance for the Early years Foundation Stage. www.publications.teachernet.gov.uk

DfE (2010), *Achievements of Children in the Early Years Profile* DFE-RR034, available online at: http://media.education.gov.uk/assets/files/pdf/t/top%2020%20research%20downloads%20-%20november%202012.pdf

—(2011), Tickell Review of the Early Years Foundation Stage available at http://www.education.gov.uk.tickellreview

Dweck, C. S. (2006), *Mindset: the new psychology of success.* New York: Random House.

Gopnik, A., Meltzoff, A. and Kuhl, P. (1999), *How Babies Learn: the science of childhood.* London: Weidenfeld and Nicolson.

Goswami, U. and Bryant, P. (2007), *Children's Cognitive Development and Learning.* Research Survey 2/1a www.primaryreview.org.uk

Hall, N. and Robinson, A. (1995), *Exploring Writing and Play in the Early years.* London: David Fulton.

House, R. (ed) (2011), Too Much Too Soon Hawthorn Pre

Kenner, C. (2004), *Becoming Biliterate: young children learning different writing systems.* Stoke on Trent Trentham Books.

Macrory, G. (2001), *Language Development: what do early years practitioners need to know?* Stoke on Trent Trentham Books.

Moyles, J. (2006), Is Everybody Ready? in Featherstone, S. (Ed) L is for Sheep. Lutterworth: Featherstone Education Ltd.

Rose, J. (2006), Independent Review of the Teaching of Early Reading available on www.teachernet.gov.uk publications

Sanders, D. *et al* (2005), A Study of Transition from the Foundation Stage to Key Stage 1. NFER available on www.dfes.gov.uk/research/data/uploadfiles/SSU2005SF013.pdf

OFSTED (2008), 'How Well Are They Doing?' www.ofsted.gov.uk, ref. 070021 OFSTED (2012) 'Moving English Forward' available at www.ofsted.gov.uk/resources/110118

Palmer, S. (2010)' Toxic Childhood: *how modern life is damaging our children... and what we can do about it.* Orion Press.

Robinson, C. and Fielding, M. 'Children and Their Primary Schools: pupils' voices'. Research Survey 5/3: www.primaryreview.org.uk

Sproule, L. et al (2005), 'The Early years Enriched Curriculum Evaluation Project: Final Report'. Belfast: CCEA www.nicurriculum.org.uk/docs/foundation/eye_curric_project/v2/year5_full_report_v7.pdf

Standards and Testing Agency, DfE (2012) http://www.education.gov.uk/aboutdfe/statutory/g00200086/2013-assessment-and-reporting-arrangements-eyfs

Suggate, S., Schaughency, A. and Reese, E. (2013), *Early Childhood Research Quarterly,* 1st Quarter 2013.

Sykes, E., Bell, J., and Rodeiro, C. (2009), *Birthdate Effects: A Review of the Literature from 1990-on* http://www.cambridgeassessment.org.uk/ca/digitalAssets/ 169664_Cambridge_Lit_Review _Birthdate_d3.pdf

UKLA (2012), http://www.ukla.org/news/story/phonics_screening_check_fails_a_generation_of_able_readers/

Vygotsky L. S. (1986), *Thought and Language.* Cambridge MA: The MIT Press.

Ward, H. (2005), 'Early Goals Out of Reach'. *Times Educational Supplement,* 21.10.05

Wray, D. and Medwell, J. (2007), 'Neatness in writing may damage the development of literacy' www.channel4.com/player/v2/player.jsp?showId=9814#

Wyse, D. (2007), 'Why Synthetic Phonics is Wrong for Our Children' www.channel4.com/culture/microsites/L/lost_for_words/phonics_10.html

Judith Dancer: Count us in! The importance of child-initiated learning in mathematical development

6

Research by the Institute of Education under the title 'Effective Provision of Pre-school Education' (EPPE) found that:

> ... in 'excellent' settings, the balance of who initiated the activities (staff members or child) was nearly equal, revealing that the pedagogy of the excellent settings encourages children to initiate activities as often as the staff. Also, staff regularly extended child-initiated activities, but did not dominate them ... freely chosen play activities often provided the best opportunities for adults to extend children's thinking. Adults need, therefore, to create opportunities to extend child-initiated play as well as practitioner-initiated group work, as both have been found to be important vehicles for promoting learning.
>
> DfES/Institute of Education (2003)

The introduction of the Early Years Foundation Stage (EYFS) for all children from birth to the end of the Reception Year offers a wealth of opportunities, but also presents huge challenges to local authorities, academics, those working in further and higher education and, of course, to practitioners and their managers.

The Early Years Foundation Stage (2008) referred to 'Problem Solving Reasoning and Numeracy', rather than 'Mathematics'. But the name change in 2012 correctly reflects that 'Problem Solving and Reasoning' occur not only in mathematics, but far more widely across all seven areas of learning and development. Moreover, mathematics is not only about numeracy, so 'Shape, Space and Measures' now has the same status as 'Numbers'. The name change reflects this shift in emphasis and reaffirms the idea of children using mathematical ideas, knowledge and an ever increasing range of strategies to: explore; investigate; identify and solve problems. Moreover, not just problems 'introduced' by practitioners, but problems which have arisen as part of everyday life, part of their play themes and real interests such as:

1 Just how many dolls can you fit into a carry cot?
2 How many more of the blocks are needed to reach the ceiling?
3 How many slices of apples each do five children get when there are eight slices? And what's more – is it fair?

The new title, 'Mathematics', recognises that mathematical skills encompass more than number and relate to broader needs and a wider context. Responding to this changed emphasis will be a key task for everyone involved with children in their early years.

Another huge challenge is addressing the inequalities in early childhood. Until Summer 2011, analysis of the Early Years Foundation Stage Profile involved the national collection of data around the percentage of children achieving 6+ on the Early Years Foundation Stage Profile for each scale of Personal, Social and Emotional Development, and Communication, Language and Literacy, and 78+ overall at the end of the Reception Year. Of course, all local authorities will continue to collect and analyse data, identify low achieving groups and plan support for individual children to raise achievement. But, clearly, this isn't simple. For example, national analysis of the Foundation Stage Profile data shows that boys are underachieving across all 13 scales, on some much more than others. All Reception Class practitioners could probably identify the scales with the largest gaps. But interestingly, and particularly relevant to this chapter, boys are significantly underachieving (between 4% and 6%) on all three scales for mathematical development. This has not always been so. Traditionally boys used to outshine girls in all areas related to mathematics. What accounts for this change? From Summer 2012, Reception Class practitioners will be making judgements of 'emerging', 'expected' of 'exceeding' for both new Early Learning Goals for Mathematics – Numbers and Shape, Space and Measures, and should be aware of underachievement for groups of children. Of course, not all boys underachieve, and when they do, environmental factors, particularly issues of poverty and deprivation, are often most decisive. But there are other, more widely applicable reasons for boys' under-achievement. Recent developments in brain research which show how boys' brains develop differently from girls' brains, are well documented. For a clear and readable summary see Bayley & Featherstone (2006). Then there is the summer born phenomenon, which applies to both genders but seems to have a worse affect on boys. But perhaps the most important factor, recognised in 'Confident, capable and creative: supporting boys' achievements' (DCSF 2007) is that practitioners (who mostly are female) need to 'tune in' far more to children's learning, in order to find out what 'turns children on to learning'. Clearly, for many children this will not be adult-initiated activities, however well planned and exciting they may appear, but it will be the experiences they initiate and develop themselves. Practitioners need to ensure that their planning for Mathematics includes both an appropriate balance of challenging adult-initiated experiences and an environment which supports child-initiated learning.

Developing a challenging, stimulating learning environment which supports Mathematics

> Children who begin their education in a learning environment that is vibrant, purposeful, challenging and supportive stand the best chance of developing into confident and successful learners. Effective learning environments are created over time as a result of practitioners and parents working together, thinking and talking about children's learning and planning how to promote it.
>
> Good planning is the key to making children's learning effective, exciting, varied and progressive. Good planning enables practitioners to build up knowledge about how individual children learn and make progress. It also provides opportunities for practitioners to think and talk about how to sustain a successful learning environment. This process works best when all the practitioners working in the setting are involved.
>
> Planning for Learning in the Foundation Stage (QCA 2001)

If children are to be given meaningful opportunities to develop their own play themes and learning interests across all areas of learning and development, including Mathematics, they should be immersed in an exciting, challenging and stimulating environment indoors and outdoors. Therefore, practitioners need to develop clearly defined and identified learning zones (or areas of provision) which support the six areas. These zones may vary, and may have different names, but the most important thing is that they exist and that both adults and children know where to go to find specific resources or to become involved in certain types of activities. To avoid repetition this chapter focuses mainly on the indoor environment. For a detailed discussion of opportunities for child-initiated learning out of doors see the chapter by Helen Bilton, which follows. (For further discussion of the learning environment, readers may also wish to refer to the chapter by Pam Lafferty in Part 3 of this book. Ed.)

Areas of provision

Over the years settings have developed organizational practices which allow them to cater for the broad range of early learning. One of these is the provision and designation of learning areas or zones. These are the ones which are most usually found, and which practitioners will want to review in seeking how they can contribute to approaching Mathematics through child-initiated learning:

- home corner and role play area
- creative workshop
- areas (or an area) for construction, sand and water
- graphics/writing area
- book corner
- malleable and tactile area
- an area for small world and imaginative play
- a space for music and sound-making
- an area which encourages and supports exploration and investigation (Understanding of the World)
- access to a computer and other resources for Technology

Some settings designate a particular space for Mathematics. Obviously somewhere will be needed to keep the resources but, rather than have a special place set aside, it is recommended that settings think about how they can create conditions and make opportunities to allow this area to permeate all the others, making it truly cross-curricular.

Of course and in any case, these areas should not be discrete and separated. There will be links and an overlap of both activity and resources between many of them. For example, the malleable and tactile zone may be combined with the creative workshop. However they are organized, these areas of provision will include core resources to form a base for activities. To supplement these, practitioners should plan to 'enhance' areas of provision on a regular basis by providing fresh stimulation and support for children as they explore, encounter and solve problems, reason, and develop their number concepts and skills. There are countless ways this can be done. The lists below are of some of the most successful tried or observed by the writer.

The home corner can be enhanced by the addition of:

- Toy puppy – with vet's appointment card, weight card, times for feeding and walks, assorted sized food bowls, dog collars, dog leads, baskets, carry boxes, dog biscuits of assorted shapes, sizes and colours, pet toys. Try leaving some important item out, to present a challenge and a problem for the children to solve. For example, omit the carry box and tell the children the puppy has to go to the vet. How are they going to transport him?
- Washing day – different sized boxes of washing powder, softener, washing line, laundry basket, various pairs of socks with different patterns, colours and sizes, clothes pegs, washing and drying machines, coins, laundry bags, handbags. A range of items of clothing offers opportunities for sorting, counting, reasoning (Who would wear this? When?) on many levels
- Message board – calendar, appointment cards for doctor, optician, baby clinic, bus tickets, timetable, post-its, take away menus, order forms, postcards, birthday cards with numerals, envelopes, shopping lists, recipes, money off vouchers, lottery tickets. Timetables and appointment calendars can be used for numeracy challenges involving telling the time and ordering (soonest/ earliest, later, latest). Menus stimulate role play and give chances to handle money. Lottery tickets require number matching

Sand or water play can be enhanced by:

- Things to catch with nets and places to store them: plastic numerals, ducks, frogs or boats with numbers on, shells, plastic fish, mini-beasts, dinosaurs, 2D and 3D shapes, number confetti, buckets, tins, wooden and plastic bowls
- Things to sieve for and things to store them in: treasure boxes and treasure, pirate ships, jewelery boxes and junk jewelery, rocks, pebbles, shells, tiny velvet, felt, muslin and organza bags and acrylic gemstones, beads and sequins, miniature baskets, stretchy socks, assorted sieves, tea strainers, plastic, wooden and metal spoons, assorted paper bags and cardboard boxes

Practitioners need to harness their own imaginations and creativity to develop a dynamic, exciting environment which challenges and inspires children. You will think of many additions to these lists, and lots of ways to enhance other learning areas. Provide the stimulus and see what the children do with it. Have some challenges, problems, questions in mind but do not over plan.

The 'workshop' approach

The workshop approach is a very effective way of encouraging children to be in control of their own learning. Practitioners should ensure that a wide range of resources are available, at child height, to enable children to make independent choices. The resources need to be stored in trays or boxes that are easy to get at and are clearly labelled with words and photographs, so that everyone knows where to find things – and, just as importantly, where to return them.

The argument for cross-curricularity, that Mathematics shouldn't be treated separately but should permeate the learning environment, has already been made. In other words, Mathemtics should not be discrete elements giving rise to activities pursued in isolation, for their own sake. Rather the task for the practitioner is to present resources and challenges that stimulate children to solve problems, using reasoning and, where appropriate and necessary, number skills to do so. Mathematics mustn't exist in a vacuum, or be tied to the workshop area where specific resources are located. It must be seen everywhere, and resources moved to support learning wherever it may be happening. Children should be encouraged and helped to combine resources from different areas, responding to the needs of their play. Children, as well as practitioners, ought to be clear about this way of working.

Developing a Mathematics workshop base

Children need opportunities to explore number, shape, space and measures independently through meaningful, practical experiences which they can initiate and develop themselves (see *A Place to Learn* (2002), for ideas and illustrations). Many of these experiences will use everyday items and things that are generally available in the setting across all areas of provision. However, children will also need to be able to call upon a range of 'specialist' resources. For example, they should have access to things to support sorting, classifying, ordering and counting. The list is endless: shells, pebbles, buttons, beads, cotton reels, conkers, fir cones, leaves, other natural resources, animals, plastic, magnetic and wooden numerals, keys, spoons, pegs, feathers, sorting circles and trays, lotto, playing cards, stickers, spheres, coloured mats and laminated cards, baskets, boxes, shiny gifts bags, purses and handbags, number lines, calculators, abacuses, commercially produced sorting equipment and collections of other interesting things, such as spectacles, sunglasses, or unusual stacking dolls or boxes.

Another list can be made of items for exploring pattern, shape, space and measures. For these activities children should have access to tessellating shapes, boxes, wooden and plastic blocks, wrapping paper, wallpaper catalogues, patterned fabric, tap-tap shapes, elastic bands and boards, linking chains, multilink cubes, magnetic, plastic and wooden 2D and 3D shapes, laces and beads of different sizes, shapes and colours, rulers and measuring tapes, ribbons, graded containers, stop clocks, rockers, mechanical timers, balances and scales, matching and track games, dominoes, height charts, and other interests things of different lengths, such as necklaces or plastic, rubber, fabric and wooden snakes.

The role of the practitioner in supporting and extending child-initiated Mathematics

We have already looked at the task of the practitioner in using space and resources to provide a stimulating learning environment, rich in challenges, creating an atmosphere that encourages exploration, speculation and discovery. But it goes further than that.

> *The role of adults is crucial in sustaining children's interest and challenging their ideas. We can extend children's thinking by raising new questions and helping them evaluate their findings. It is particularly helpful if, when children are engaged in an activity, practitioners model the key vocabulary using descriptive and comparative language – ask open-ended questions about how things work and why things are happening.*
>
> Skinner (2005)

In a later chapter Jane Cole discusses the complex and dynamic role of the early years practitioner in detail. It encompasses planning, based on children's learning needs and interests, identified through observation of children and discussion with their families, and which ensures children have space and uninterrupted time to follow their learning interests. It includes identifying opportunities for learning throughout the environment (as well as recognising those things which inhibit learning). And particularly, in this as in everything, it involves setting an example. A lively, enquiry-based and questioning approach will not be encouraged unless practitioners themselves show inquisitive behaviour by asking, thinking aloud and speculating.

In doing this they will also be introducing and modelling the use of mathematical language.

Modelling, of course, should not replace or override the children's ideas or dominate what they are engaged upon. The answer is in achieving an appropriate balance. The EPPE research referred to above found that freely chosen play activities often provided the best opportunities for practitioners to extend children's thinking, and that in the most effective settings practitioners regularly extended child-initiated activities without dominating them. (DfES/Institute of Education, 2003) Experienced, effective practitioners know when to intervene and extend children's learning. They also know – and in many ways this is a harder skill to master – when to stand back, watch, listen and note.

Conversely, observations of practitioners working in the least effective settings often show that a disproportionate amount of adult time and effort is spent in planning and 'delivering' adult-initiated activities aimed to promote Mathematics. This can mean that when children are not 'targeted' for an adult-led activity, they are left to 'get on', by choosing from a range of experiences of variable quality. Ineffective practitioners often fail to plan appropriately for children's learning needs and interests, miss assessment opportunities and also fail to observe children engaged in the sort of self-initiated play in which they are generally functioning at their highest level.

The EPPE research also found that good outcomes for children are linked to early years settings that provide adult-child interactions that involve open-ended questioning to extend children's thinking. The sad fact is that often many questions that practitioners ask are 'closed' (and often 'testing') questions that have a single right answer (which is what the questioner expects and wants) and which can usually be answered monosyllabically. For example,

- What colour is the car?
- Do you want beans or peas?

That very often applies, too, to questions asked about Mathematics:

- How many beads are on the tray?
- If we have two apples and eat one, how many are left?

Some children avoid such questions and on occasions will actually avoid adult contact if they feel they will be tested. These children are often those who have had experience of giving the 'wrong' answer. It is they who are most at risk of underachieving. However, if children realise that adults are asking questions because they are actually interested in them and what they are doing and that there are no 'wrong' answers, they are more likely to engage in positive interactions with practitioners. Here are examples of open questions that reveal the questioner's interest in the processes, rather than the outcomes, and encourage breadth of thinking:

- What was the first thing you did with the large boxes? and next?
- What will you need to make a necklace longer than the yellow one?
- Which do you think could be the best sized bed for the doll?
- What can we do to remember how many magic beans are in the tin?

Some of the best examples aren't questions at all, but rather invitations to become involved in a discussion ('I wonder why the big box feels lighter than the small one'), solve a problem ('We need to think of a way to make sure we all get the same number of carrot sticks'), experiment ('I think that if we put both the dinosaurs in the boat it will sink'), or simply talk ('Can you tell me about the construction you have made?').

Finally, we should not forget the effectiveness of success and of positive reinforcement. This is another reason why closed questions are so limiting. If the child produces an answer different from the one expected it is patently wrong. Experiencing a lot of wrong answers can engender feelings of error and inadequacy, to the extent that the child may avoid answering all together. In contrast, some of the least expected, off the wall answers to open questions are often the most interesting. It is crucial that practitioners ensure that children's early experiences of Mathematics are successful. Positive dispositions and attitudes are more important than skills and subject knowledge at this stage. We must encourage children to be inquisitive, interested, eager and motivated. It is our duty to be engaged in their learning and help them to maintain a positive view of themselves as learners and problem solvers, developing increasing confidence in their achievements and their ability to learn. If we get these things right, children will view Mathematics as pleasurable and something they want to engage in.

Bibliography and references

Bayley, R & Featherstone, S. (2006), *Boys and Girls Come Out to Play*. London, Featherstone, Bloomsbury Publishing plc.

DCSF (2007) 'Confident, capable and creative: supporting boys' achievements – Guidance for practitioners in the Early Years Foundation Stage'. London: Department for Children, Schools and Families.

DfES/Institute of Education (2003), EPPE Technical Paper 10 – 'Case Studies of Practice across the Foundation Stage'. London: DfES.

Lewisham Directorate of Education (2002), *A Place to Learn – Developing a Stimulating Learning Environment*. London: London Borough of Lewisham.

QCA (2001), *Planning for Learning in the Foundation Stage*. London: Qualifications and Curriculum Authority.

Skinner, C. (2005), *Maths Outdoors*. London: BEAM.

Skinner, C and Stevens, L (2013), *The Foundations of Mathematics -An Active Approach to Number, Shape and Measures in the Early Years,* Bloomsbury.

Stevens, J. (2007), *Maths in Stories*. London: BEAM.

Helen Bilton: Setting the scene for child-initiated learning out of doors

7

We all have our own ideas about education, what it should be and what it should do. So here is mine. Education for me is about deciding what you wish to produce and then working out how to do it. I want to produce people who think for themselves. My overriding desire is that we create a society where each individual looks at any given situation, thinks about it and then makes a decision. Sometimes that decision may be uncomfortable and may cause problems, but the key factor is that the person has thought about it and believes it to be the right course of action.

So, for example, I consider speed cameras to be a sign of our failure as a society. The need for cameras to enforce speed limits means that a majority of people can't think for themselves, can't see the connection between speed and safety, and need controlling. It means that some people cannot look at a road and think, 'This is a built up area and the safest speed is not more than 30mph'. No, these people just drive as fast as they want until there is a speed camera (or an accident!). They haven't learnt to do their own thinking and need someone or something to control their behaviour on the road.

So how can we develop a thinking society? As many people before me have concluded, the place to start is with children. Put simply, you get children into the habit of thinking, reasoning and working things out for themselves. The best way to do this is to allow them to do things, to enquire, to experiment, to grapple with problems and ideas and to come up with solutions. This process should be held in much higher regard than merely regurgitating received information about, say, the Tudors or knowing the difference between a metaphor and a simile, important though these things may be. It is about running with an idea and sometimes finding a solution and sometimes not, sometimes having people to help, sometimes not. This is the basis of child-initiated learning and it leads to children being able to think for themselves. That is why it is so important.

What does an environment for child-initiated learning look like?

Of course, the processes I have described can take place almost anywhere – in a school or setting or at home, indoors or out. What is needed is a physical environment and an approach which says to the child, 'Lots of things are possible. Whatever you wish to do, you can – as long as it doesn't put you or anyone else in danger – and we will make sure you have the time, resources and support to do it'.

Here are some examples of what I mean.

Two girls wanted to be S Club, and they practised singing and dance routines outside. They decided to put on a show and went to the technology table where they made tickets. They went round the nursery selling tickets to everyone. Finally, they put on the show in 'Wembley Stadium', which they had built themselves from a netball goal, with an old curtain draped over and small chairs inside, thereby appearing to be the covered part of the stadium.

Another example, using the same piece of equipment, involved an obstacle course. Two children decided to make an obstacle course, using anything they could lay their hands on. They didn't have a great deal to work with, but the netball goal laid horizontally became a high jump, they used pegs as markers to run around and a skipping rope laid on the ground to make a tight rope. Once they had designed their obstacle course they built it and tried it out. Some things didn't work in the way they wanted. The pegs weren't in the right places, the rope sagged too much. So they adapted it and tried it again. When they were satisfied with the improvements they invited friends to join in.

A third example is provided by two five year olds who built a home in a tree house. After 'living' in it for a little while they came upon the problem of how to get their mail. They had no letter box at the base of the tree, and they couldn't expect the postman to climb up the ladder to deliver their letters. Besides, it was their tree house, and they wouldn't have wanted that. So they made a post box from a shoe box, with a slit cut out for the letters. They attached it to a length of washing line, to the other end of which they tied a bell. They hung the washing line over a branch of the tree, with the bell at the top, in the tree house, and the 'letter box' at the bottom. When the postman put letters into the box he tugged on the rope, the bell rang and the residents of the tree house pulled up the box and collected their mail.

What did these children learn? They learnt that their ideas worked. They learnt to work together, to get on with each other, to negotiate, and compromise when necessary. They learnt that their ideas had value and were respected by the adults, who helped them find the resources they needed to apply their solutions. They learnt to use their initiative and to adapt – 'I haven't got this, but this will do instead'. They learnt to persevere, that failure isn't a problem but an opportunity to be even more inventive. They covered lots of areas of the curriculum – adding up, counting out, estimating, using numbers in context, speaking and listening, reading, writing, measuring, understanding causes and effects, the list goes on.

Looking to, for example, the work of David Wood (1998), or Liz Wood and Jane Attfield (2005), there is clear evidence of the link between how we set up our environments and what we get from children. 'Learning becomes more efficient if children become consciously aware of the processes that are involved in learning, and how they can gain control over those processes.'

Was any of this important to the world beyond the setting? Of course. We all have to get on with others. Much of the time and effort of children and adults is devoted to trying to get on with other people and persuading them to do the things we think are important. And yes the grappling, the failures, the ability to keep going are important. There are many examples of the effectiveness of perseverance in the face of problems. Consider James Dyson, originator of a number of inventions, including the bag-less vacuum cleaner. His story is one of determination and of a creative response to the difficulties he encountered. He experienced many failures in evolving his designs, getting them produced and convincing sceptics that he had something worthwhile. Many people tried to discourage him, but he didn't give up. Did this all come from playing outside? I have no idea. But Dyson does admit he grew up believing he was different, and embracing his differentness. He met people who thought in unusual ways. He met engineers who valued art and design as well as building things. So a number of factors came together to help him develop into the innovator he became. Perhaps we should call our young people not child-initiators but inventors, designers, engineers, because with all their creations they are designing, building for purpose and creating new objects. As Dyson himself is reported to have remarked, 'Enjoy failure and learn from it. You can never learn from success'. Not universally true, but challenging enough to be worth thinking about.

How do you set up an environment for child-initiated learning outside?

Let us start by agreeing what not to do. Do not have lots of bikes, plastic wheeled toys, or fixed climbing equipment. The effect of these is simply to encourage predictable, and usually adult controlled behaviour. What can you do with a bike in the outdoor play area except ride it round and round? Yes, you can pretend it's a bus or a truck or a car, but ultimately you just go round and round. This may be good for physical development but is not much of an intellectual challenge. In some settings which, with the best of intentions, have been equipped most lavishly, children learn little more than how to get a high status toy quicker than someone else. This will not lead to being a good citizen.

The second thing to avoid is a too rigid pattern of organisation. The outdoor area should not be a timetabled environment, where children go in turn for half an hour a day, to run around frantically if they are boys and potter on the immoveable equipment if they are girls. It should be a resource, constantly available (even in poor weather), a space which children can employ when they need it, just as they might use a home play area or a book corner.

Having considered what to avoid, what are the things we should do? Firstly, we need to foster amongst the adults in the setting an attitude of mind which believes that anything is possible and values the qualities and potential of all the children. We need to cultivate the feeling that we are surrounded by great people – inventors, designers, engineers and sculptors; they just happen to be younger than we are! Secondly, the outdoor space should be open and clear, not filled with lots of clutter. Thirdly, within that space children need a wide range of materials, so that when a design idea comes the materials are available, and when more are needed the children know they can go and get them. Or if the exact thing they need is not available they can find a suitable alternative. Examples of some of the things you might make available are carpet squares, pieces of heavy material of differing sizes and shapes, ropes, pegs, broom handles sunk in cement in plastic pots, canes, guttering, plumbers tubing, boxes and so on. Fourthly, children need as much time as possible outside, preferably combined with the flexibility to access the indoor environment when they need to, so that if what they are doing requires them to use something that's normally kept inside – perhaps, for example, to make something at the technology table, they can get at it.

Of course, when the weather is fine you can always move resources such as the technology table outside, but don't forget that children sometimes need a bolt hole. They need somewhere to go to take a break from all that thinking, or to reflect on what they have been doing. I suspect James Dyson had to spend lots of time pacing about thinking, discussing his ideas with others, or maybe just sitting at a table or in a quiet corner to enable his brain to cool off and re-charge itself for the next bout of creative activity.

If this ethos and environment are new to the children they will need support in being creative and inventive, and it will be useful if adults themselves model the sort of creative behaviour that they want to encourage in the children. It's a bit like being asked to say what rhymes with cat. If you don't have the concept of rhyming or any experience of what rhyming involves, it's tricky. So initially the adults may generate their own ideas and work on them, involving the children as part of this process. This not only demonstrates the sort of inventive and creative thinking you are aiming to promote but also shows that you approve of this way of children behaving in your setting.

But isn't this incompatible with child-initiated learning? No, not if it is simply a means to an end. Start by thinking about things children could make. Tell them about these, and collect the resources and materials with them. Then design and create with them. Having supported them a number of times, the children will begin to come up with their own ideas. As this develops you can reduce your own involvement so that the children can pursue their own ideas without you. However, don't rush them. Allow plenty of time. This isn't going to take days, but weeks. Another way to get things started is to offer ideas in the form of photographs. Mount a selection of photos taken of the children's designs, inventions, models, or from real life in small photo albums. You can also include unusual pictures from other places that you think will trigger ideas and stimulate imaginations. As children flick through these images they will come up with anecdotes, speculations, stories, ideas. Let the talk flow, prompting and extending where you feel appropriate, bringing in additional resources as seems appropriate. Respond positively to all suggestions, and if children come up with something impossible (e.g. too dangerous, too expensive) don't reject it out of hand. Talk about it with them and help them to see the potential and implications of their ideas.

Time spent in this way is a means to an end. It is not about adults setting up ready-made scenes, which children have to play with whether they like it or not. Tovey (2007) found a small group of practitioners she worked with spent collectively 20 hours 'setting out and putting away outdoor resources'. It is a much better use of the time to collect as many and varied resources as possible, arrange them in some sort of storage system, properly labelled using words and pictures and accessible to children, which they can use at their will. Just because you have set up the resources for playing out the 'Goldilocks and the Three Bears' story outside doesn't mean it is necessarily going to inspire anyone. Doing the thinking for the children won't get them thinking for themselves, in this situation or any other.

Finally, resist the temptation to be over tidy. An early years outdoor area is not a suburban garden or a park, but a place where children can invent, discover, create, recreate, adapt, whether it be a castle, a pet shop or a new style of lawn mower. So think of an effective outdoor environment for child-initiated learning as a workshop. And like all workshops, it will sometimes look messy – at least to an outsider who is not fully aware of what is going on.

What else does the adult do?

The essence of child-initiated learning is that it is an approach which permeates the whole curriculum. It is a way of thinking, not something you time-table or 'do' at certain times of the day or week. So any aspect of the outdoor area could be affected. A child could come across fungi (see Bilton, 2004) and wish to find out more about them. This is a good example of child and adult working in partnership. It is child-initiated because the discovery and the interest comes from the child, although as fungi are risky it requires the involvement of a knowledgeable adult. Child-initiated learning has many different aspects, and quite simple – and apparently unimagi-native – beginnings can lead to enquiry, problem solving and creative expression. So the S Club girls started with imitating but actually moved into designing tickets, building a stadium and organising a show. The obstacle course began when the children started to move the goalpost out of the way. At that moment the idea of the obstacle course started to ferment in their brains. The postbox idea came from two children simply climbing into the tree house and starting to play.

What is most crucial is what the adult does before all the play begins. It needs to rest on a clear and firm philosophy of education. Even with all the central guidance, requirements and initiatives which have impacted on the early years sector in recent times, there is still scope for practitioners to put their own mark on the environment for teaching and learning. That is why The Effective Provision of Pre-School Education (EPPE) (Sylva et al, 2004) project can come to the conclusions it does about some classes being better than others. We all have the same broad curriculum to deal with, but it is how we approach it which makes the difference to the children. So my philosophy of education is about creating people who are independent thinkers and who can stand by their ideas. This means I have to create an environment where children can be independent in action and thought, where they are valued for their thoughts and ideas, where struggling is seen as a virtue not a sign of weakness. So much of the adult role is about creating an ethos for this style of learning; it takes time, dedication and effort.

Next steps?

Get rid of the bikes and all the brightly coloured wheeled toys. Start to collect heavy material, carpet squares, boxes, fabric, ropes, pegs, tubing, guttering, canes, broom handles, netting. Buy A-frames, planks, child-sized ladders. Take photos and put them into albums. Talk to the children and model how you want them to be and tell them why. Talk to them about great inventors, designers, architects, philosophers and artists. Work with them, alongside them and watch them. Discuss their designs and inventions, whether they be an imaginary play scene or a discovery in the woods. Talk to them beforehand when they might be having ideas, while they are creating, and afterwards to reflect upon their learning and discoveries. Be patient and value their creations. Whitebread (2012), argues that' 'a child who has experienced the excitement of finding things out for themselves or of solving problems is learning to take risks, to persevere and to become an independent, self regulating learner.' (p.12) Lastly, trust children. They are quite capable of becoming the next generation of thinking adults.

Bibliography and references

Bilton, H. (2004), *Playing Outside*. London: David Fulton Publishers.

Sylva, K., Melhuish, E., Sammons, P., Siraj-Blatchford, I. and Taggart, B. (2004), The Effective Provision of Pre-School Education (EPPE), 'Project. Findings from Pre-school to end of Key Stage 1'. London: DfES.

Tovey, H. (2007), 'Playing Outdoors.' Maidenhead: Open University Press.

Whitebread, D. (2012), *Developmental Psychology and Early Childhood Education*. London: Sage Publications Ltd.

Wood, D. (1998), *How Children Think and Learn*. Oxford: Blackwell.

Wood, E and Attfield, J. (2005), *Play, Learning and the Early Childhood Curriculum*. London: Paul Chapman Publishing.

Wikipedia, (2007), http://en.wikipedia.org/wiki/James_Dyson

Part 3: Special issues

Sue Palmer: An inconvenient truth: early childcare has to be upfront, personal and real

8

As I walked my dog in the park the other day, we bumped into a group of children. Three nursery workers were exercising their young charges … on leads. And while my dog had a minder all to himself, the careworkers' leads divided into three leather straps, each of which was tied to the waistband of a toddler; nine small children, each in harness.

Of course, children need outdoor exercise, and physical safety is important. But the sight of these poor tethered infants, blundering, bewildered and bumping into each other, made me want to weep. They needed loving grown-ups to hold their hands, chat about what they saw around them, and stand guard while they toddled around the park finding out for themselves by looking, touching and interacting with the world they found there.

Not only does it seem shameful on a human level for small children to be given less time and attention than my family pet, but it's counter-productive on a scientific level too. I have spent most of this decade researching modern childhood, wading through books on cognitive psychology, papers on neuroscience and endless reports on childcare and childhood well-being. And the conclusion I have come to is that it is impossible to ignore the massive body of evidence showing that – if children are to grow up bright and balanced enough to contribute to society – more than anything they need in the first couple of years the personal time and attention of a loving adult.

Indeed, the most influential book on child development, 'The Scientist in the Crib', by three of America's top scientific experts (Gopnik, Meltzoff and Kuhl, 2001), tells us that babies and toddlers are themselves like mini-scientists, primed to explore and explain their world. And for this, they need high levels of personal support.

The comparison between infants' self-initiated learning and scientific enquiry is startlingly appropriate. From birth, babies are hard-wired to act like mini-scientists observing, testing with all their senses, hypothesising and making logical connections. Within six months they appreciate many characteristics of the material world. By one year they can categorise objects and phenomena by quite complex rules. By 18 months they've sussed out cause and effect, and are beginning to use simple tools.

It took the human race hundreds of millennia to get that far, and babies – if they're lucky – do it in less than two years.

Luck comes into it because babies are born without control of their bodies and are therefore dependent on assistance from someone older. A good 'personal assistant' can provide access to all the equipment and data the baby needs at exactly the right moment. This avoids frustration, as well as making sure the baby is safe, secure, comfortable, well-fed and watered at all times. So the quality and commitment of the assistant is critical, and will have an effect on the rest of the baby's life.

But she also has another important function. (As the assistant is usually female, I'm going to call her 'her' and the scientist 'him' from now on – just for the convenience of the pronouns. But please bear in mind that gender is irrelevant on both sides). As well as investigating the physical world, mini-scientists also need to find out about the social world they will one day inhabit. So they need to investigate people. Each 'scientist' therefore studies his 'personal assistant' – she becomes his specimen.

The moment a scientist is born, he stares into his assistant's eyes. To begin with, he's unable to see anything very clearly, but within a matter of weeks he develops enough control of his ocular muscles to enable him to focus on near objects. So he studies his assistant's face more closely, and begins trying to imitate her facial expressions and her body movements. At the same time his hearing is developing, and he soon tunes into the sounds his assistant makes as she looks at him, plays with him, changes him. He begins to try to imitate these noises. By the time he's about a year old, he's well on the way to speaking her language (they call it 'mother tongue') and, with her help, he'll soon be walking around like her too. What's more, through constant access to her mind he's on the way to a seriously important deduction – one that separates human beings from all other animals.

If everything so far has gone well, during his second year on earth the mini-scientist works out that the assistant and he must both be able to think, independently of each other. Human beings have minds – they can plan, review, consider, imagine. Philosophers and scientists are only just beginning to get to grips with the origins and huge significance of what they call 'mind-mindedness'. The toddler isn't able to rationalise or put into words the concept that humans have different minds and different wills, but he soon comes to realise that what his assistant wants and what he wants are sometimes different!

By the age of two, the small scientist is so aware of other people's minds that he's conducting frequent experiments to find out vital information to help him establish his future role in society. What is acceptable behaviour between humans? How far can he get his own way? How far will he need to cave in to the requirements of others? These tests and experiments can be very trying, for both sides. We've long called this period 'the terrible twos' – and it requires all an assistant's patience to see the scientist through.

So throughout his vital quest to understand the world, our mini-scientist needs personal help. He needs close, consistent and reliable encouragement and maintenance. The chances of providing such personal support in an institution – particularly poorly-funded and over-regulated institutions like many of today's nurseries – are very low indeed.

In an institution each mini-scientist competes for attention with a lot of other scientists, who are also engaged on the frantic search for knowledge but who are all at slightly different stages in the proceedings. With the best will in the world, institutional helpers are unlikely to be tuned into his wave length, unless they are not only very good indeed but also have the time to be able to concentrate their entire attention on one or two children.

What is more, if there are different nursery staff on duty on different days (or at different times of the day), it stands to reason that some of them will not know the child well. Moreover, if they are being regulated by Ofsted they will often be too busy with paperwork to give the young scientist the time he needs to facilitate his enquiries. As one frustrated nursery worker said to me, 'I'll be down on the floor, playing with the children and having a great time. Then suddenly I'll think "I'd better write that down"... and then the moment's gone'. When this happens job satisfaction decreases, leading to high staff turnover and making it even less likely that each infant scientist will have the constant, consistent personal assistance he needs to learn about his world and the people in it. Indeed, child psychologist Steve Biddulph has recently said that 'quality nursery care appropriate to young children does not exist. It is a fantasy of glossy magazines' (Biddulph, 2006).

But there is another, even more important reason why a mini-scientist needs the time and attention of an individual personal assistant. This reason is catalogued in the vast literature on attachment theory, which underpins much developmental psychology and conventional psychotherapy, as well as a lot of considerably more ancient wisdom. With any luck for the future of the human race, the little scientist and his adult assistant will fall in love.

Scientists desperately need to know about love, because it makes them more human. It's one thing to know that the person looking after you has a mind, and getting interested in learning how to manipulate it. But actually caring about what is going on in that mind, wanting to be able to understand her point of view, is what will turn the young scientist into a fully-fledged human being. The social, responsible behaviour we require of a citizen is rooted in empathy. If a child's discovery of mind-mindedness happens as part of a loving, empathetic relationship, the more capable that child will be of developing genuine empathy ... and the more social, responsible and caring he will be as a citizen.

What is more, the realisation that his faithful assistant loves him is also priceless because, for the rest of that scientist's life, he will have the security of knowing that he is loveable. This gives him the self-esteem and self-confidence to face the challenges of life and withstand its catastrophes. It helps him make an effective and creative contribution to the society he lives in, whatever his particular talents.

This is what made me want to weep at the sight of those poor tethered infants in the park. Institutional care doesn't just look less pleasant than the sort of one-on-one personal attention I give my dog. In terms of human development (the gradual inter-twining of cognitive, social and emotional growth), it cannot possibly cater for all the needs of children in their first two to three years. To rear a well-rounded, resilient human being, the person (or people) in charge of a child for the first two to three years of life must be personally involved in a loving relationship with him or her.

For the most fortunate of us, of course, the mutual love affair leading to empathy – and thus to social behaviour – is with a parent. If we're very lucky, it's love at first sight (and this happy event is commemorated in countless paintings of the Madonna and Child). The work of developmental psychologist Colwyn Trevarthern on 'the dance of communication', which begins the moment a mother gazes into her baby's eyes, illustrates the importance of a reciprocal human gaze in developing a responsive parent-child relationship.

Eye-contact appears to be deeply important: in his book *The Cradle of Thought* developmental psychopathologist Peter Hobson shows how the reciprocal gaze develops into a 'triangle of inter-relatedness' – mother at one corner, child at another, the world at the third – so that the child's gradual dawning of understanding about the world is embedded in a comforting, loving relationship (Hobson, 2002). For the cover of his book Hobson chose a William Blake engraving of a mother holding her infant in her gaze, while he looks out at the audience. Beneath the picture Blake has written, 'Teach these souls to fly'.

Research makes it clear that it doesn't have to be the mother who bonds with her child, and this is confirmed by the experience of many adopted and fostered children. There is no need for a blood relationship, just a personal one. Now that the requirements of national and domestic economies mean that women are needed in the workplace as well as in the home, this is just as well. If the demands on a modern mother mean that she lacks the time or the opportunity to be her offspring's assistant (or perhaps simply doesn't want to), a good substitute can do the job just as well. Another family member, a nanny or a childminder can give the child love, time and personal attention just as well as its mum.

But the fact that love matters so much raises another important point for those caring for the under-twos. Just as an institution is an inadequate substitute for a loving human being, so is a screen. The experiences a mini-scientist needs are first-hand ones – real interactions with the real world and real eye-contact with real people.

Until 30 or so years ago, there was no alternative to this reality – those caring for babies or toddlers had to engage with them personally at all times. It was not possible to leave them in front of a television, video or DVD. This has always, of course, been a huge responsibility and some carers – especially those who felt deep abiding love for their charges – have throughout the ages risen to it more successfully than others. With increasing wealth and smaller families throughout the 20th century, more parents and carers had time to devote to the task. But since the 1980s the explosion of screen-based entertainment means children can now be left in the company of electronic babysitters. Babies will naturally be attracted to and will watch moving patterns of colour and light. Like many adults, they are often hypnotised by screens and will gaze at them for hours. There is a temptation to leave them to do so; after all, they seem to be interested and enjoying themselves. Therefore the amount of screen-based entertainment aimed at tiny children is growing by the day, with television programmes aimed at the under-threes, a dedicated 'Baby Channel' on satellite TV and shopfuls of DVDs with titles like 'Baby Einstein'.

All these products give the impression that electronic entertainment is an adequate substitute for human eye-contact, attention and warmth. However, there is not a shred of evidence that electronic babysitters aid brain development, even though some of them have very beguiling titles and are blatantly marketed at aspirational parents, who buy them under the impression that watching them will do their baby good. On the contrary, a growing body of research suggests that the regular exposure of young children to extended periods of screen-watching may do long term emotional and psychological damage. Yet although the American Academy of Pediatrics has recommended for many years that children under two should not watch television at all, this message has not got through to carers. A Scottish study recently found that two-year-old children, raised in a screen-based world, are now as sedentary as adult office workers. Early years practitioners throughout the UK can testify to young children's increasing lack of conceptual, social and linguistic skills in the last couple of decades. And it doesn't take much imagination to see the connection between this and the malaise that affects many of our young people in their teens and beyond.

It's a terrible irony that, as 21st century science uncovers the immense importance of child-initiated learning from the moment of birth – and the need for loving adults personally to support this learning – society increasingly discourages individuals from providing that support. Governments urge parents to put babies and toddlers in nurseries so that they are free to go out to work. Big business and the media sell us technological alternatives to first-hand human interaction which are promoted as being actually better than anything a parent might be able to provide at home. We end up tending to the needs of the economy today, rather than nurturing the citizens of tomorrow.

This 'inconvenient truth' about the needs of tiny children could in the long term be every bit as significant for the human race as climate change. In an increasingly crowded and complex world, tomorrow's citizens will need all the cognitive skills, emotional resilience and empathy they can muster to help keep humanity on the straight and narrow.

Bibliography and references

Gopnik A., Meltzoff A. N., Kuhl P. (2001), *The Scientist in the Crib: what early learning tells us about the mind*. London: Harper Perennial.

Hart, Betty and Risley, Todd R. (1995), *Meaningful Differences in the Everyday Experience of Young American Children*. Baltimore: Brookes Publishing.

Herschkowitz, Norbert and Herschkowitz, Elinore Chapman (2004), *A Good Start in Life: understanding your child's brain and behaviour from birth to age 6*. New York: Dana Press.

Biddulph, Steve. (2006), *Raising Babies: should under 3s go to nursery?* London: HarperThorsons.

Gerhardt, Sue. (2004), *Why Love Matters: how affection shapes a baby's brain*. London: Routledge.

Hobson, Peter. (2002), *The Cradle of Thought*. London: Macmillan.

Reilly, J. J., Methven, E. *et al.* 'Health Consequences of Obesity', *The Lancet*, January 2003.

Thomas, Susan Gregory. (2007), *Buy Buy Baby: how big business captures the ultimate consumer – your baby or toddler*. London: Harper Collins.

Jan Dubiel: Tiaras may be optional – the truth isn't: the Early Years Foundation Stage and accurate assessment

9

What is the function of assessment? Progress in any learning environment relies on accurate and reliable data or information. Otherwise, how can we know the stage the learner has reached and plan opportunities for his or her further development? Assessments or records which are useable, meaningful and give a clear picture of the stage the child has reached are an indispensible component of effective pedagogy.

What assessment does – or should do if it is to have any value in helping us to meet the needs of individual children and prepare for their next steps – is provide us with an accurate description of the child at a point in time and at a particular phase in his or her learning. It must be a dynamic and sophisticated tool that enables us to make sense of those key positions in time and learning. It must help us to understand the complexities of children's development and, crucially, both guide us in the direction their learning is taking them and indicate what we can do to support, encourage and extend it. And, most importantly, it must also provide us with this information in ways that make it easy for us to use it. Assessment data that is too complicated or dense to be readily understandable is useless.

Assessment, then, is a tool. However, we need to be aware that this process – the use of this 'tool' – does not take place in a vacuum. Assessment cannot be neutral or value free. The act of making an assessment is itself strongly driven by a set of influences, realities and contexts which determine its nature and shape. Making assessments is subject to our own perception and understanding of what we see as an adult. It is based on our own agendas and preoccupations, mediating children's activity through our own values and principles, defining what is considered important and driving the provision, interactions and support that follow. Assessment is based on our own versions of the truth and the evidence we gather constructs our own concept of actuality; from this we decide what part the child's reality plays. So these things go hand-in-hand: we make assessments of children because we need to, as a vital component of responsible pedagogy; we need them in order to plan and provide for their development and learning; but we must be aware that these assessments are also subject to our own system of beliefs and our own views of what should or could be.

So it is important to consider what kind of values might surface here when taking into account how an effective pedagogy – one that recognises children as diverse yet universally rich and competent learners – should shape our approach to assessment, and the potential pitfalls of it not doing so.

Let us consider three factors which affect assessment. To begin with, we need to be clear about what the Early Years Foundation Stage (EYFS) guidance means by 'the unique child'. The phrase in this context refers to the individuality of the child's learning and development. There is no short cut to this, and however convenient it might be to simplify the reality of children's learning, treating everyone the same in order to produce a neat and tidy data set, it will inevitably result in that most useless of exercises, the collection of data that is unusable and meaningless. As Margaret Carr suggests,

> ...assessments, in trying to 'make sense' of data and turn in a plausible story, always run the risk of over simplification: losing the rich and often ambiguous complexity of young children's behaviour.
>
> Carr, 2001

Secondly, we need to think about the role and impact of the learning environment in which the assessments take place, and the type and quality of the interactions that occur within it. In what the EYFS guidance describes as an 'enabling environment', children demonstrate all aspects of their learning, and engage continually with and feed from the context in which they are working. In doing so they reflect their own understanding and also use it as a platform for further development. What we make of the child's interactions with the environment are strongly value driven, and are determined by the third factor: outcomes. The outcomes that we decide are important are the ones we search for, and those are the ones we find. Conversely, what we decide is unimportant is hardly noticed or even ignored. So the outcomes of the assessment are to a great extent predetermined when we decide what we are going to look for and how we are going to look for it.

All this leads to two inescapable, and hopefully obvious, principles: firstly, assessments need to be accurate; they need to be true and reflect the reality of children and their development. Secondly, they must be usable.

This begs several questions. How do we do it? How can we glean and gather information from which we can start to understand a child's development? How do we establish and define the behaviours we wish to assess without affecting the outcomes of the assessment? How can we ensure that the assessments we make are both useful to us and inform the next stages of learning.

Arriving at answers to these questions is not easy. For one thing, we know that children's learning is complex and highly individual. We know that they don't always 'play the game' in acting in the way we want, or in telling or showing us what we might want to know at a particular instant. Margaret Carr notes that, 'Our experience tells us that children are not always eager (ready or willing) to learn in the domain that we are willing to teach.' (Carr, 2001). We also know that young children's reality is 'of the moment', densely coloured by the specific 'desire' or 'thought journey' that is accompanying it at the time. It's like trying to get a good photograph of something that is moving unpredictably and very rapidly. If only it would keep still, I could manage, we think. But keeping the child's learning still would destroy it, as well as rendering the assessment worthless. Trying to pin down exactly what busy children are doing, and the learning they are demonstrating in any formal or clinical manner, has always been highly problematic.

If we want the truth, if we want a reality that can be used and is consistent with the values we need to consider, then it has to be sought, and the eminence of observing children's self-initiated activity is thereby established. But we also need to be careful in defining what this means. 'Self-initiated' means just that; it means being able (and allowed) to pursue those densely coloured desires and thought journeys of the moment. It is also strongly dependent on the surrounding ethos, the explicit and implicit values of practitioners and settings. Children are sharply attuned to these and will modify their own realities according to their perceptions of what is promoted, encouraged, permitted and tolerated in their environment. It is only when they really know that what they do will be valued and celebrated for itself that children will have the confidence to initiate activities in the first place. So let's be clear; child-initiated learning isn't simply a child being busy in the role play, sand, construction or indeed any other area of provision. It is about the context and environment within which that activity happens, it is about a child deciding the route that their thinking will take, and responding to sensitive adult interaction and support to progress and develop their learning.

In the fifth century BC the Greek philosopher Plato is reputed to have made an important observation about play. He said, 'You can discover more about a person in an hour of play than in a year of conversation'. More recently, Vicky Hutchin noted that 'It is only through gathering evidence of learning in an eclectic way that we can get a true picture of a child's real achievements, whatever their age and stage in education ... In the early years context, to gather a holistic picture of the learner, learning in a range of play situations needs to be observed' (Hutchin, 2003).

In those play or self-initiated activities, children are themselves. They follow their own agendas, they draw upon the environment and upon the support of and interactions with adults. In these situations, children demonstrate what they can really do because they need to and want to, in order to realise the outcomes and overcome the challenges they themselves have defined and set. This is learning and development at its most potent and meaningful, but more than this, it provides the best opportunities for making assessments because at these moments the reality of the child's knowledge, skills and understanding is most evident. What is more, assessments made here are likely to be most accurate – and therefore most useful and usable – because the situation in which they are made is real, and because it derives from the child's inner motivation and demonstrates their true understanding. They are usable because they dramatically identify the child's learning and development at a particular point in time.

Effective assessment, then, is about establishing 'the truth' of the child's reality. And the proper use of assessment is to inform the next steps in learning by determining how the needs of the child can be best supported and provided for. I have tried to show above how this is mediated by the values we hold. It is also affected by our understanding of how to describe it. Because this is difficult it has often been dodged. Historically, the early years has had an inferior status in the educational firmament. One result of this has been the spawning of a pseudo-scientific industry dedicated to producing precisely the kinds of clinical measurements that devalue and reduce children's development and learning through testing that is supposedly objective, but which in fact is simplistic and formulaic. These testing methods have been devised in response to a requirement to produce easily understandable data about children, preferably in numerical form, which pretends to enable performance to be measured and children compared. They do not have as their starting point how best to describe the complexity of an individual child's learning. Instead they rely on the universal application of a set of rules. These assessment methods are frequently the result of the early years being treated as a 'bolt-on extra' to some other assessment and tracking device that already exists in the organisation, and which needs data from the early years for its evidence base. Too often the creators and proponents of these systems don't have the expertise or understanding to apply them properly to young children, nor the honesty to admit this. I find it incredible that there are still assessment systems used in some schools that – without any sense of irony – claim to measure a child's learning and development by instructing them to point to an object on a picture or repeat a word. Worse still, these specific, socially loaded and frankly bizarre actions are somehow supposed to be predictors of future development and attainment. There is a small child in a Hans Christian Andersen story who would have something to say about this…

Contrast these unimaginative and mechanical assessment methods with the most effective observational assessment, rooted in the ongoing reality of everyday practice. At the heart of this is the expertise of the skilled and reflective practitioner who, as she observes, 'logs' those priceless examples of thought, understanding and skills which the child, often unaware of the practitioner, demonstrates in their self-initiated activity. These nuggets of information, gathered almost subconsciously, enable the practitioner to develop a view of the child's achievements. This is information not to be dryly recorded and filed, but to be used when modifying provision, and when planning opportunities and future interactions with that child. All practitioners are continually building up a huge wealth of this information and it is imperative that they are not distracted from this. Invariably the bulk of this assessment evidence is from self-initiated activities, the point of reality, the moments in which children truly show what they can do. It is here that effective practitioners see or hear the impact of their provision and interaction, not merely in the demonstration of specific pieces of knowledge but in the processes the children employ, the thinking they demonstrate and the manner in which their learning is used and expressed.

The Early Years Foundation Stage Profile was revised in 2012 to reflect the new EYFS. It remains a statutory record for the end of the EYFS and within its process values above all the nature and outcome of children's self-initiated activity. It asserts that:

> "the majority of evidence for EYFS profile judgements will come from the practitioner's knowledge of the child gained from observation of self-initiated activities." (S&TA p10).

In assessing the Characteristics of Effective Learning; the learning 'behaviours' that underpin the content enable children to apply their knowledge and skills, it states that

> "Accurate assessment of these characteristics depends on observing learning

which children have initiated rather than only focussing on what they do when prompted." (S&TA p10).

It also refers to the nature of 'embedded learning and secure development' which is again wholly dependent on opportunities for children to self-initiate their activity and take 'ownership' of both the process and the outcome.

Of course, this guidance has a philosophical base and reflects a particular view of children's learning. Its ultimate aim is to create a 'data set', so the assessment it discusses needs to be accurate and meaningful. Without the prominence given to observing children's self-initiated activity, which is the key strand of evidence for making judgements, it cannot claim to reliably represent attainment within the EYFS. Moreover, if assessment is an embodiment of values, the guidance clearly makes some bold assertions. Practitioners are required to make a series of judgements that cannot be made in any other way than through systematic observation of child-initiated activity. There is no realistic, formal method of assessing whether a child is 'confident to try new activities' or 'show sensitivity to other's needs and feelings'. These can only be assessed through observation, and only when the child initiates actions that may demonstrate them. Practitioners acquire the knowledge they need to make this judgement over periods of time, adding constantly to their experience of the child and building a mental picture of his or her development – not always recording it formally. Nor can descriptions of capabilities and behaviour such as 'expressing themselves effectively' be assessed without the practitioner's knowledge of how this happens spontaneously in situations the children create themselves. This really can happen only in contexts where child-initiated activity is promoted, encouraged, supported and celebrated as the most valued approach to learning. The judgements can be secure only if the environment, interactions and ethos of the setting implicitly and explicitly support them. The revised EYFS Profile handbook refers to this as 'responsible pedagogy' and its necessity in enabling 'each child to demonstrate learning in the fullest sense'. How else can practitioners make accurate, informed assessments of, for example, whether a child 'represents their own ideas, thoughts and feelings through design and technology, art, music, dance, role play and stories'?

When we assess we do so for a purpose. Irrespective of the later uses of assessment information, its main purpose in the early years is to inform the practitioner and to help shape future provision. It is 'live' information at the heart of effective practice, recognising individuality and embodying the values of principled, effective practice. It is not that observing children's self-initiated activities is an easier option for undertaking assessments – it is more likely to be the opposite of this – but that this is the most reliable means of discovering what children really know, truly understand and actually can do.

About the author

Jan Dubiel is the National Development Manager for Early Excellence that provides Early Years training, consultancy and support for local authorities, schools and settings. He has significant experience teaching Nursery, Reception and Year 1 and is a highly regarded consultant. Jan was Programme Leader for the EYFS and EYFS Profile at QCDA and had national responsibility for the profile's implementation and moderation.

Bibliography and references

Carr, Margaret. (2001), *Assessment in Early Childhood Settings*. London: Paul Chapman Publishing.

Hutchin, Vicky. (2003), *Observing and Assessing for the Foundation Stage Profile*. London: Hodder Education.

Standards and Testing Agency (S&TA) (2012) *Early Years Foundation Stage Profile Handbook*.

10 Jane Cole: Our role as adults in enabling independent learning

Everything we do as early years practitioners needs to be based on our belief in children as independent learners. Everything we do also needs to be based on our understanding of how babies and young children learn. And we know that they learn through active play and first-hand experiences, as appropriate for the age and stage of child. Exploring, using all their senses, children make sense of the world around them. So the environment – their world – must keep our children safe from serious harm as well as being an exciting and challenging place for them. Besides setting up and resourcing the environment, we need constantly to review and refresh the learning opportunities it offers. We can do this with the users, and need to enlist the involvement of all in these tasks, including the children themselves. Unless our actions are underpinned by these beliefs and understandings, the opportunities for the children are impoverished. They will continue to develop as independent learners but it may be in spite of some of the adults around them, rather than as a result of their support. Children have an amazing resilience, which we need to nurture, not narrow.

So child-initiated learning starts from a base of warm and trusting relationships with the children. Having formed these, we need to introduce them to the opportunities on offer. The children will then make their own choices and come up with creative solutions and new connections.

The process is completed by sensitive observation of the children as they play in this enabling environment, so that we can assess their interests, needs and development. These assessments support and extend the children's independent learning by informing the practitioner's further, personalised planning and prompting the introduction of new materials and experiences.

All this keeps us busy. However, we should not underestimate the importance of the final key, which is for us ourselves to act as a resource. The knowledge, skills and experience of the adults closest to them are the young child's major support, and the first port of call when looking for information, know-how, or simply another pair of hands to help with a particular task.

Sensitive intervention will open up a dialogue with the children. This adult/ child interaction, which will be founded on our beliefs about and approach to early learning and informed by knowledge and an understanding of the individual child, is an essential context of and support for children's progress. One thing I believe that we need to become more comfortable with is silence; not grim, tense anticipation but relaxed and secure silence which is itself a means of communication. Initiating interactions and responding to children in order to create a meaningful dialogue is a high level skill for the adults. However, it is essential for us all to work on developing this during our careers, because of its crucial nature in enabling a child to scaffold his or her learning.

To demonstrate the application of some of these key elements in this chapter we will share two stories. They illustrate aspects of provision and demonstrate responses by adults that make possible children's independent learning and progress. These stories demonstrate the adults' belief in the children as learners and their under-standing of how they learn. It is clear that they have established, and continue developing, positive relationships with the children – demonstrating their personal interest in them and confidence in their abilities as learners. One further point: in both these stories the learning is enriched by a constant flow of shared information between home and school, which reinforces for the children this positive partnership.

Both stories were noted during autumn 2007 at a children's centre in south London. This centre was a maintained nursery school which, as part of a pilot some years ago, had added the provision of a family room to enable work with babies, their carers and families. There are long established links with the local community and the centre benefits from a stable staff. The centre has invested in the learning environment, in and out of doors, over the years and its resources are continually reviewed and refreshed.

The first story begins with the children settling into the nursery class and two boys becoming friends. They played a lot outside, and their key persons supported their engagement with the wide range of learning opportunities always on offer in the outdoor environment. A wooden garage, cars and a road mat were among the resources made available, and the boys started to use planks stored alongside to extend the roadway. They tested each section with their cars.

After a while the boys ran out of planks and wanted to extend the roadway further, so they used a range of other materials available in the garden. Other children watched and started to join in. The boys pressed into service all sorts of bricks and shapes to make up their roadway. There was mathematical thinking and tessellation going on all around the garden! Other children got involved and began balancing along the block roadway, following each other from beginning to end and then starting again.

All this was observed by the children's key person, who noted the co-operation and innovation that was going on and the

various skills and behaviours the children were displaying. She supported the learning by commenting as the boys continued the construction, by modelling some mathematical language relating to length, shape and position, and by using

positional/descriptive language such as straight, turn, back. The provision indoors and outdoors supported and extended the children's interest in pattern making.

Parents got involved too, by listening to the stories from the children and sharing observations with the practitioners. The learning story was photographed and the sequence of events described. This was then put in a folder and attracted lots of interest from parents and children. The parents of the two boys who started the play were pleased with the evidence of their children's social, mathematical and design skills. This was an eye-opener for one mother in particular, who had the impression that her son spent his whole time at nursery riding round the garden on a tricycle! The story was copied and put into his special folder, which he proudly took home and shared with his extended family. Both families reported that the children were interested in continuing to develop this interest at home, and they were able to develop these links in their learning.

All the children had found learning experiences that matched their interests and extended their skills – motor skills in constructing and using the roadway, language in the discussions with the other children who became involved, mathematical skills and skills of design and technology. The school staff were particularly pleased with the social behaviour of the two boys, and thought it admirable that they did not protest when other children started to build and develop what was, after all, their roadway. They seemed happy to allow different types of involvement and for other children to use what they had made in different ways. For the boys the construction had started out as a road, but other children adapted it for other uses; for example, an obstacle course, adding small challenges such as pyramid blocks. One boy with a communication disorder also became interested in the construction, and he spent time sitting on the planks and watching.

Staff had developed resources in the garden over a period of time, and the children were used to using these. Among the most popular were some supports which had been made by setting wooden ladders in buckets filled with concrete. To these they had added some plastic pipes and guttering which children could employ to link the ladders together. The boys saw the additional possibilities of these, and started 'driving' their cars along this aerial roadway (see the picture on page 98). This extension provided opportunities for them to explore forces and friction as they experimented with different slopes and junctions.

In this story we see how the positive relationships, the support of practitioners and parents, and the rich, continuous provision of resources in and out of doors gave the children confidence and enabled them to progress their learning in a range of areas. It is important to identify the examples of different elements of staff knowledge and expertise apparent in this approach, so that we can understand why and how the support of the adults was so effective in extending the children as learners. It is this focus on processes which creates a pedagogy that enables the best learning outcomes.

The family room at this centre provides a base and a resource, drawing in parents and carers of children from a few days old up to three or four. It runs daily drop-in sessions each morning and afternoon. Many children enter the nursery class at three, so families are able to make regular use of these facilities over several years as their children grow. Health and social care professionals are regularly available in the family room, and they introduce families who would benefit from the provision. The learning environment consists of a large indoor playroom, a children's bathroom (also with adult facilities), a baby sensory room and rooms for holding training and meetings. The family room links to the nursery garden, with a large circular sandpit which is covered so it can be used throughout the year. Additional grassy areas, slopes and various wheeled toys are well used, and seasonal activities, such as digging and planting, capture the attention of the children and their carers and engage their interest. Local families are pleased that, living in this built-up area, their children are able to spend time playing actively outdoors.

The staff are effective in engaging adults with the children both in the drop-in sessions, family learning linked sessions and in the focus groups. A recent group was led by a dietician, and the families were keen to share the healthy eating recipes that their children had started to enjoy. They are running cooking sessions in the family room, photographing and putting together a recipe book. This facilitative approach, engaging and extending the parents' knowledge and skills, mirrors the work with the children noted earlier in this chapter.

As part of their ongoing evaluation to ensure the provision meets the needs of the users, the staff put together a number of case studies each year. Other support professionals, such as social workers and health visitors, work with the families to build a profile of each child. These document their learning and development both at home and in the setting. Some of the families who make regular use of the provision also join in these shared stories. The following is one of them.

Caitlyn is nearly eight months old now but has been coming regularly to the family room drop-in sessions with her mum since she was only six days old. By now she feels very secure in the setting. She is actively exploring the world around her and using all her senses. She sits independently and reaches for objects around her. The staff in the family room noticed that she was particularly drawn to some shiny metallic cloth. As they watched they were unsure if it was the look of the material

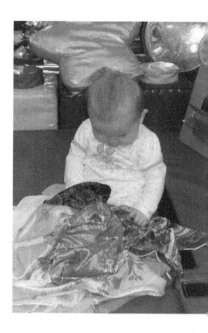

or the noise it made that was attracting and sustaining Caitlyn's interest and exploration. Following some more observation at home and in the play sessions the adults decided to offer Caitlyn a choice of two sound-making toys. Caitlyn reached for the rain stick and rolled it towards her. She held it in one hand, watching and listening intently as the beads flowed through. Then she explored it with her mouth. She focused on turning the stick over to see the brightly coloured beads bouncing through. And though she dropped it in her lap, she picked it up and continued to explore.

Caitlyn sustained this interest for quite a long time. When they saw that her attention was starting to fade, the staff gave her some fabric. She started to hide the rain stick underneath. Then she lifted up the material to find it again. Her mum had told the staff that they had started playing peek-a-boo at home, and as they watched they could see Caitlyn repeating and extending this game with the rain stick and the fabric.

In this story we see many examples of good practice in the way the adults stimulated and extended Caitlin's independent learning. The richness of the opportunities, and the appropriateness to children of Caitlin's age of the resources provided in the family room, are regularly reviewed and enhanced in the light of children's changing needs and interests. Sensitive observations are shared, and in some cases carried out jointly with parents. The adults not only look, listen and note the children's responses; they engage in dialogue with them. The progress of each child is shared and celebrated.

These stories show how, by providing an enabling learning environment, keeping it constantly refreshed, observing the active learning of individual children and enhancing the provision through opportunities for sensitive interaction between children and adults, independent and child-initiated learning is enabled and enriched. They also provide powerful illustrations of the role of adults. The involvement of skilled, observant, resourceful and sensitive adults enables the child to build on previous learning and equips him or her with the confidence to continue the learning journey. And these key adult qualities are not restricted to the practitioners. Given the right resources and support, parents and carers can work n partnership with the practitioners. It is adults working together – having the development of the child at the centre of their thoughts and actions – that make the difference to outcomes. Supported in this way children show us what powerful and creative thinkers they are. It is this that makes our time with them so exciting and rewarding.

Pam Lafferty: Child-initiated learning – a view from HighScope **11**

What does child-initiated learning look like?

It is usually helpful to start by establishing a basis of understanding, so let us begin with a definition. What is child-initiated learning? The short answer is that it is 'what it says on the tin'. It is a situation where the activity from which the learning comes is originated by the child. The idea comes from the child and arises out of his or her individual and unique thoughts, questions, plans, or intrinsic motivation to learn.

The intrinsic motivation to learn is what characterises human kind. Some of the other higher mammals can and do learn, but for them learning is a means to an end. It has a clear purpose: getting food or shelter, defending against attack, protection from the environment. As far as we know it is only human beings who learn simply because they want to, because they want to know how or why.

Intrinsic learning can be described in more everyday speech as what makes you tick, what floats your boat or, as an Ofsted Inspector suggested to me to add to my collection of phrases, what tickles your pickle! So if intrinsic learning is something children do anyway, why is it so important?

To begin with, in the current climate of raising standards and passing tests, intrinsic motivation is often given only brief recognition. Sometimes it seems that what is rated, particularly in the higher echelons of education, is the mere ability to find and absorb information and re-present it. However, in the Early Years Foundation Stage (EYFS) guidance there is a requirement that observations of children are to be made in child-initiated situations. It follows that practitioners will need to know how to support such situations, and how to observe, understand what they are seeing and hearing, and use those observations in their planning.

Let us look at an example. As Ben crosses the carpet he sees how the sunlight shining through the window has created a small triangle of light on the floor. He bends down to look at it. It interests him. He puts his hand on the floor and sees that the triangle now shines on his hand. He is fascinated. He hurries off and returns with a small plastic triangle, which he places exactly over the triangle of light. It matches, and he smiles and claps his hands. A truly 'eureka' learning moment!

An observer, sitting near by, has watched the little scene and writes down what she has seen Ben do. His short burst of activity and enquiry covers a range of learning outcomes and goals:

- matching shapes
- understanding of the world
- science, maths, higher level thinking, etc.

Best of all, it was a chance event. Ben just happened to notice the shape made by the sunlight. The experiments that followed came entirely from him. He wanted to know and the process of finding out absorbed him. Because it was his, he was learning at a time he was ready, and so he was able to absorb the experience and widen his understanding. The adult observed it and is now in a position to think about how to support this learning going forward.

The practitioner may provide selections of differently shaped objects, more opportunities to observe light and shadows inside and outside, or maybe have a conversation about the discovery. These ideas would be offered as choices for the child to take up if he chooses. However, he may well have moved on to something else by tomorrow! In the words of Jo Williams, a pedagogue in Cheshire, 'Surrender yourself to the moment, take that moment and add to it, but resist the temptation to develop it into a topic'.

That is the nature of giving full value to child-initiated learning. It can't be planned and written down neatly on a piece of paper before the event, because you don't know what is going to happen and if you have a detailed plan that covers every minute of the day you won't be able to give time to that special learning moment.

It can be uncertain and scary for practitioners to have large periods of time in the day when they are to 'expect the unexpected'. They need to have a clear supporting framework in place to enable them to help the child to develop and make the most of the opportunities he or she creates. So how do we support child-initiated learning and give it full value in our daily encounters with children and their unique learning paths?

The first requirement is a knowledge and understanding of child development. If we know the stages each child will pass through we will be better equipped to judge 'where they are and what comes next' as we accompany them on their learning journey.

In the HighScope approach to learning a number of elements combine together to enable the practitioner to support the child's learning effectively.

- Active learning
- Learning environments inside and outside
- A consistent yet flexible daily routine
- Plan-Do-Review
- Adult/child interaction
- Encouragement

Active learning

Active learning is the principal element of the HighScope approach and has five main ingredients: materials, manipulation, choice, language and support.

Children should have access to a variety of interesting resources, including a large number of 'free and found', open-ended materials, which they can use in different ways. It is important that these materials are freely available to children throughout the day. Secondly, they need to be free to explore, handle, move and work with the materials. Next, they must be able to choose. Children need opportunities to set their own goals and select not only the materials, but also what to do with them and who to work with. They will want to talk about the materials, the choices they have made and what they do with them, and this will lead them to communicate, verbally and non-verbally, about what they are doing. Finally, adults support children's efforts and help them to extend or build on their work by talking with them about what they are doing, by joining in their play and by helping them to solve problems that arise. Support also comes from the wide choice of materials and from their peers. Many adults believe that as long as children are handling materials they are engaged in active learning, but this is only part of the story. While the manipulation of materials is essential, that on its own does not create an active learning situation. For true active learning to occur all five ingredients are necessary.

Active learners become engaged in play and problem solving because they themselves choose to do so. Remember Ben and his sunlit triangle? Motivation theorists suggest that children choose to become engaged in activities and interactions that are enjoyable, related to their current interests and that allow them to experience feelings of control, success and competence. It has been put very well by a number of influential thinkers.

David Weikart, Founder of the HighScope Educational Research Foundation has written, 'Action alone is not sufficient for learning. To understand their immediate world, children must interact thoughtfully with it'. Or as Aristotle put it, 'What we have to learn to do we learn by doing'.

The environment for learning

While children will initiate learning almost anywhere, there is a better chance of it happening if the environment is created to support it. Child-initiated learning is more likely to occur in well-defined interest areas which satisfy these criteria:

- Different types of play can occur
- The areas have names that the children can understand; e.g. 'writing and drawing' rather than 'graphics' (which, believe it or not, I have seen used as a label in a room for under fives). A favourite of mine comes from a Children's Centre in Gateshead, where the two and three-year-olds had named the role play area, the 'tendy' area, because you go in there and 'tend' to be something.
- There are visual boundaries between the areas
- Traffic flow has been considered
- The interest areas are modified as children's interests change

Within their environment children must be able to choose the materials they are going to employ. There should be a range available that reflect their interests and developmental levels, and which can be used in many different ways; e.g. coloured bricks may be used to build or to 'cook' within the home corner. The materials available should also reflect the experiences and culture of the children in the room, and reflect human diversity in unbiased ways.

The materials must be easy for the children to find and use. They need to be at child height so they are within reach. They need to be stored consistently in the same place, so that the children get used to where to look for particular things. Shelves and containers should be labelled in ways that children can understand; e.g. pictures, outlines, silhouettes, words. Good labelling supports a 'find, use, return' process, which not only encourages good habits but will help to keep things available for use by everyone. These things are obvious, but it is surprising how often one or more of them is overlooked. If children do not have swift and ready access to the materials they need we run the risk of their interest waning and the moment and the opportunity will be lost. Think about the outcome if Ben had not been able to locate, easily and quickly, the plastic triangle. He would have missed that unique chance of experiencing the essence of the shape and of apprehending how the beam of sunlight passing through the window created it.

The daily routine

When does child-initiated learning take place? The answer is, anytime. And often it can't be predicted. Children's ideas need to be supported throughout the day. Within a HighScope daily routine, which is consistent yet flexible, there is a balance of child-initiated and adult-initiated elements. All the adults and children understand clearly whether they are engaged in one or the other. What you will not see are times of the day where there is a mixture of the two, i.e., children choosing what they do, while at the same time adults call them away to engage in something the adult considers important, or adults anchored at a focus table which all children are expected to visit. The message given to the children here is that the adult's activity is more important than the work the child has initiated. Flexibility does not mean allowing everything to happen all the time. It means planning opportunities to make the very best use of the environment and circumstances, and following a consistent approach.

Plan-Do-Review

In HighScope settings all the adults are involved with the children at 'Plan-Do-Review' time – or as a child in Kent, when asked to name their favourite time of the day, called it 'Plan do and with you'. She understood the concept of the adult as a supportive partner!

Plan-Do-Review is the longest section of the HighScope day and truly child-initiated. The child thinks and considers what they would like to do, where they would like to do it and which other children they might involve in their work. Then, having done it, they look back over what happened, who did what and how things turned out.

Adult-child interaction

The process followed during this period of the day is enriched by the adult. In their role as a partner and by their understanding of strategies identified by the High/Scope approach they sustain shared thinking. Rita Weiss has devised a framework for this, which uses the acronym SOUL.

Silence
Observation
Understanding
Listening

SOUL, combined with putting oneself on the child's level, both physically and intellectually, enables the practitioners to come closer to the child-initiated play. She or he can then begin to understand what is happening and might either be invited in by the child, invite themselves in or decide they are not needed and withdraw to engage with another child or children.

Once the practitioner has entered the play they are able to use other strategies to support the learning: For example,

- use the materials the children are using and let them take the lead
- match their pace to the child's pace
- take turns in play and conversation
- follow children's leads by listening and responding
- use comments as conversational openers (usually more effective in inviting the child to say more than lots of questions)
- acknowledge what children say to encourage them to continue the conversation
- accept children's explanations
- use questions sparingly and make them genuine, i.e. ask questions that you don't already know the answer to. Questions are most effective when they tap into the interest and thinking of the child

Encouragement

Do we support children's initiated learning by praising or encouraging? This is the element of the HighScope approach which practitioners find most difficult to understand, and then even more difficult to implement. It is the one which supports child-initiated learning more than any other single element. Commonly, current thinking supports a climate of praise. The HighScope approach believes that practitioners should encourage rather than praise, as research tells us these strategies have very different outcomes for the child.

Looking to definitions from the *Shorter Oxford Dictionary* one finds:

- Praising: expressing in speech approval, admiration or honour
- Encouraging: making sufficiently confident or bold to do a specified action

Praise comes from 'outside' the child and is the act of someone, usually the adult, judging what the child has done. This can in the long term make children very dependent on approval. Encouragement on the other hand is about engaging the child from the inside and tapping into what makes them tick, thus creating a desire to learn and, more importantly, to keep on learning.

So, to illustrate the point: If the practitioner says 'Good boy, you washed your hands' it results in the child thinking, 'If I wash my hands I can get the admiration of this adult'. On the other hand, if the practitioner says, 'You washed your hands,' it enables the child to reflect on their capability and think, 'Yes, I can wash my hands by myself any time I want to!'

Offering encouragement, not just praise, is a difficult concept and in a chapter such as this I can only raise awareness. I struggled for a long time to make it part of what I do and others have followed in that struggle, but once you are aware of the difference and you see at first hand the effect it has on children's confidence and motivation, you will want to employ it as a key principle in the way you relate to children.

In conclusion, in settings where the HighScope approach is adopted, adults provide many opportunities for genuine child-initiated learning, through active learning, a carefully considered environment, a consistent, flexible routine, Plan-Do-Review, quality adult/child interaction and encouragement without praise.

References

HighScope training materials both from the US and the UK. Contact the following for more information.
HighScope GB
The Sue Hedley Nursery School
Campbell Park Road
Hebburn
Tyne and Wear
NE31 1QY

www.high-scope.org.uk

e-mail: marina@highscopegb.org

12 Theodora Papatheodorou: Bilingual learners

Much of the earlier part of this book has emphasised the value of the interaction between children and supportive adults. Child-initiated learning is cemented and developed through regular and frequent conversations. Of course, these are only of value if all parties to the conversation can understand each other. English is the medium of communication in virtually all early years settings, and will be the first or only language of many practitioners. However, for many others – and for many more of the children – it may not be. That is why it is important at this stage to consider the particular needs of bilingual learners, and how they can be supported.

Increasingly in the early years more children than ever speak more than one language; that is, they speak English, the formal language of their education, in the nursery or at school, and another language at home. Urdu, Hindi, Turkish, Cantonese, Spanish, Portuguese, Greek, Polish, Arabic are just a few of the many languages spoken among UK citizens and residents. Early years practitioners who educate and care for these polyglot children often experience uncertainties and concerns about their practices, which may have long term effects on children's education and well-being. Similar dilemmas are also faced by parents, many of whom like their children to learn English and, at the same time, maintain the mother tongue. However, supporting bilingualism is not an easy task (Suto-Manning, 2006; Fishman, 1996; Arnberg, 1987).

This chapter aims to address some of the issues and complexities of bringing up and educating young bilingual children in a child-focused way. It aims to do so by highlighting the importance of sensitively supporting the development of more than one language at the same time at home and in early years settings, and offers some pointers for how this can be done. For the sake of clarity, borrowing from Gregory (1996) the term 'bilingual learner' has been taken to refer to a young speaker who develops competence in more than one language with the same level of competency and fluency as does a native speaker, and who is able to identify positively with parts of both language groups and cultures. The term 'home language' will be used interchangeably with the terms 'mother tongue' or 'heritage language' to refer to the language that is spoken at a bilingual learner's home (Browne 1996).

Bringing up and educating bilingual learners: Issues and complexities

Cameo one

The boy arrived at the nursery school with another boy of the same age (around three and a half years old), accompanied by a woman in her mid-30s. Initially, he played with the boy with whom he arrived, but soon he moved on to another group of children who were playing in the construction area. He smiled. Then he picked up a block. He showed it to other children. He said something and he repeated it a few times (it seemed to me he was explaining what he was doing – I understood he was speaking Spanish). A girl responded, saying 'brick … this is a brick'. He repeated 'brick' and smiled.

Later he drew a picture and scribbled underneath it. He approached me and showed me the picture. He pointed at the writing and said, 'Rodrigo'. Before I responded, he showed the picture and pointed at himself and repeated: 'Rodrigo'. I understood that that was a picture of him and his name was Rodrigo.

The nursery teacher approached me. She explained that today was Rodrigo's first day in the nursery. She said that he had arrived in England from Mexico the previous day (Sunday). She commented that Rodrigo has no language at all. (I assumed she meant Rodrigo has no English language!)

(Excerpt from a researcher's notes)

Cameo two

When we arrived in England, David, my son, was three years old and spoke our home language fluently. He joined the local nursery school and, for almost eight months there, he refused to speak in English. When I initially tried to use picture books to introduce to him some basic everyday vocabulary, he refused to join in, asking me not to speak these stupid things. I kept buying picture books in English, as I did with books in our home language, and left them among his toys. I bought tape-recorded songs, picture and talking books. I would listen to them when my son was playing with his toys. I avoided making the point that he should listen, but I knew that he did.

> *Then, one day, returning from the nursery school, he started talking in English. In full and well-structured sentences he described the visit of a farmer into the nursery school. He explained that the farmer brought his animals to the nursery for the children to see them. He did so because everyone in the nursery school was very good and well-behaved.*
>
> *A year later his English improved, but his home language declined. Despite my efforts to speak to him in our home language, English took over. I would speak in our native language and he would reply in English. To my surprise, during a visit back home he switched from English into our home language to speak to his grandparents, cousins and relatives. However, he started having difficulties communicating fluently in the mother tongue. This made me determined that he would speak both languages equally well and fluently. This was a decision that in practice was proved not to be an easy task.*
>
> (A mother's account)

Is the mother tongue a deficiency or an asset?

In cameo one, the nursery teacher referred to Rodrigo as having 'no language at all' because he did not speak English! Perhaps the nursery teacher's comment was unfortunate, but it also demonstrates how limited proficiency in English may be seen as a handicapping condition or deficiency (Ruiz, cited in Kerper Mora et al. 2001). Research, however, has shown that the mother tongue is an asset that cannot be ignored. Mastering the mother tongue means that the child already knows that language has a structure and form and that communication has its own rules and conventions that go beyond verbal expression (Whitehead, 1997). This was vividly demonstrated by Rodrigo when he joined the group of children in the construction area. Knowing one language means that the learner can pick up a second better and faster because he does not need to start from scratch (Tse, 2001). The mother tongue then forms the child's linguistic, cognitive and social capital and is the foundation for emergent bilingualism. The question is whether the mother tongue will flourish or gradually become redundant.

Becoming bilingual

Whereas some children, like Rodrigo, may be natural and forthcoming communicators, these attributes do not apply to every child. In cameo two David, a fluent and competent speaker of his home language, was reluctant to speak in English. In fact he did so only when he felt competent (and therefore confident) in the new language. David's case raises questions for early years practitioners who work with and assess children using standard intended learning outcomes. Had David, for example, been assessed in language and communication skills before he was ready to speak English he would have failed all the criteria for the anticipated learning outcomes. This would not have provided a proper indication of his capabilities in language, and perhaps a label would have been attached to David that might have carried with it the consequences of a self-fulfilling prophecy.

Cameo two also shows that as the language of the host country takes over as a main medium of communication the home language declines. In David's case it was a little while before this happened, but once it started it happened very quickly. The tendency of English to dominate is reinforced by the fact that English has increasingly become the 'acknowledged world language' (Whitehead, 1997) and as such offers opportunities for competing in the world economy and technology.

The importance of bilingualism

Most parents who have their origins in non-English cultures are determined that their children shall not only learn English, but at the same time maintain fluency in the home language. There are excellent reasons for this. The importance of maintaining the home language is linked with children's culture, heritage and identity, and the development of positive relationships with elders and relatives. Learning the language of the host country is about accessing education and about assimilatiing into and integrating with the dominant culture. This has the practical advantages of increasing opportunities for employment, raising cultural awareness and appreciation, and enrichment (Papatheodorou, 2007; Papatheodorou *et al.*, 2006). Additionally, research has shown that bilingualism is beneficial more generically by being linked with children's enhanced cognitive and metalinguistic abilities and the promotion of flexible thinking and information processing (Cavallaro, 2005; Bialystok, 1991; Bialystok and Ryan, 1985). Researchers argue that by operating with at least two language systems, which gradually become interdependent and nurture each other, young bilinguals are better equipped to handle thought and experience (Baker 2000; Cummins 2000).

Yet there is much ambiguity among parents about the place of the mother tongue within the majority culture of the host country. As the functional use of the mother tongue is limited mainly to within the family, it tends to become gradually sidelined. Despite the best intentions of parents to maintain the mother tongue, the language of the host country gradually dominates (Papatheodorou, 2007).

Clearly, bilingualism is a complex issue, presenting challenges and dilemmas for both parents and educators. Informed early years practitioners may like to remember and remind parents that:

- The mother tongue is an asset – not a deficiency
- A child who masters the mother tongue and its communication rules will learn and master another language, too
- Learning another language may be approached in different ways and at a different pace by different children – growing competence and confidence is important
- The mother tongue is important for children's awareness of their own culture, the development of their own identity, and for cross-generational communication and positive relationships within their family and community
- The language of the host country is important for accessing education, for assimilation and integration, and for cultural enrichment
- Bilingualism leads to enhanced cognitive abilities, flexible thinking and better information processing

Most parents are committed to the learning of the mother tongue; others may be ambivalent and less clear about its value. Speak to them and help them to understand the importance of bilingualism.

Supporting bilingual learners

Understanding the issues and complexities surrounding bilingualism may be a step in the right direction, but early years practitioners may be with a group of children where several different mother tongues are spoken by different children. How can they support and address the needs of all these children and every child individually, in order to advance and enrich their social and cognitive capital while at the same time safeguarding their personal growth and well being?

The two cameos have shown that child-initiated, playful and interactive activities that are mediated by others (e.g. other children in the case of Rodrigo, the mother in the case of David) are the best means of stimulating and encouraging language learning. Child-initiated learning starts from children's interests, and because of this it maintains their attention and engagement. It also provides the context for communication, negotiation and action and its non verbal, physical and emotional clues facilitate meaning making. For example, the play materials in the construction area provided Rodrigo with the context and immediate experience to communicate with other children and speak aloud his first words in English; his drawing became the visual aid to introducing himself to the researcher. Similarly, David's mother became the facilitator for the second language by supporting his play with appropriate resources and tools (e.g. picture and talking books, tape-recorded songs).

The actions taken by both Rodrigo himself and by David's mother reflect the underlying principles of good early years practice. We know that planning for learning in the early years should start from, invest, and utilise children's prior knowledge and lived experience; such experience being mediated by knowledgeable others helps children reach their full potential (Bredekamp and Copple, 1997; Vygotsky in Van der Veer and Valsiner, 1991; Bruner, 1990; Vygotsky, 1986).

Tuning into the child's experience

Monolingual early years practitioners, and even those with a bilingual background, are unlikely to be familiar with all the languages that may be represented in an early years setting. Similarly, the setting itself is unlikely to have resources to reflect such linguistic diversity. Therefore, it is important to acknowledge and capitalise on the linguistic skills, experience and potential of bilingual learners and to be prepared to learn from them as well as to teach them (Whitehead, 1997).

The first step is to tune into children's immediate experiences of child-initiated learning. Role play, mime games, practical activities (e.g. eating, washing, tidying up, cleaning etc.) and sorting and matching activities offer opportunities for practitioners to introduce new vocabulary by labelling objects and actions. Starting from concrete, familiar and known experiences, practitioners can gradually introduce unfamiliar, unknown and abstract concepts and ideas.

Investing in the functional use of language

The best way to facilitate language learning is to concentrate on its functional use. Bruner (1990:73) argues that language mastery can be achieved 'from participation in language as an instrument of communication'. Child-initiated learning activities provide concrete referents, contextual and multi-sensory cues (e.g. visual and auditory cues, hands-on involvement, body language, facial expressions), and association with emotions – such as amusement, hesitation, excitement – for the learning of new words (McWilliam, 1998).

Establishing shared meaning

It is important to remember that learning a new language is not simply a matter of learning new words. Children also have to grasp new concepts and make sense of a brand new world (Gregory 1996). To achieve the internalisation of the language which is vital to understanding its meaning, it is important to employ multi-modal and multi-sensory representational symbols, such as pictures, stories, puppets and modelling. Creating a learning experience that is child-initiated, sensory, fun and emotionally warm, by responding to the child's pace and drawing his or her attention to sounds and available cues can enhance children's capacity to make meaning for themselves (Tassoni, 2007).

Creating multilingual inventories

It is also an important aspect of support for bilingual learners to show genuine interest, respect and curiosity in their mother tongue. Whilst early years practitioners introduce new words in English, they can also ask children to repeat them or even write them down in their mother tongue. They can take the opportunity to create bilingual and multilingual inventories, supplemented by children's own drawings or relevant pictures to provide links with visual text. Naming everyday objects and activities (e.g. words about food and eating, clothing and dressing, cleaning materials and cleaning) may be the starting point for the creation of such multilingual inventories, which when completed can be strategically placed in relevant areas of play (e.g. kitchen, home corner etc.) to reinforce bilingualism. Parents and older siblings can offer the linguistic and even practical help to both children and early years practitioners to develop these resources.

The development and use of multilingual inventories shows children our appreciation and respect for their mother tongue. It also introduces mono-lingual children to cultural and linguistic diversity and encourages them to become aware of, and perhaps explore, contexts which might be unfamiliar to them.

Making your own books

Children's drawings can also be used for the creation of bilingual and multilingual books. Encouraging children to talk about their drawings, early years practitioners can take the opportunity to write down in short sentences children's description of the picture. In this way, the visual stimulus is turned into verbal and written text that expresses the meaning which the child gives to his picture (Graham, 1998). Parents can be invited to do the same thing in the mother tongue.

Collecting individual children's drawings over time and binding them together will give them their own personal books whose reading can be shared with parents, siblings, other children in the nursery and early years staff. Technology makes it possible to scan or take a picture of children's drawings, which bound together thematically will create a library of multilingual books whose reading may be shared with all children of all language backgrounds.

Making a library of 'home-made' multilingual books has an additional value because they can be used to capture and document the child's achievements in more than one language and so contribute to assessment and the future planning of learning (Barratt-Pugh, 2000).

Encouraging language mixing, language switching and interlingual lexicon

Of course one of the concerns is whether this process can be confusing for children, leading to language mixing, that is the mixing of words from both languages in a single utterance. Language mixing is common among emergent bilinguals; children who are developing two languages at the same time will sometimes mix words from them in a single sentence. In time it gives way to language (or code) switching; that is, swapping from language to language when talking to speakers who are competent in all the languages being used (Whitehead, 1997; Arnberg, 1987). A variant of this is the combination in one word or phrase of elements from more than one language in order to make up a term to convey a concept common to both languages but for which there is no term in one of them. An example is the Greek word for 'fish and chip shop'. Fish and chips are not a traditional Greek dish, so there is no word for fish and chip shop in the Greek language. However, there is a word for fish shop (*psaradiko*). To convey 'fish and chip shop' the term 'fishadiko' has emerged among Greek migrants, combining elements of both English and Greek (*see* Papatheodorou, 2007).

Practitioners will see children doing the same sort of thing, when bilingual learners merge prior and new experiences and knowledge to create new vocabulary which derives from the two languages and cultures. Indeed, the introduction of 'interlingual lexicon' (as this is called) exemplifies Whitehead's (1997) assertion that 'Bilingualism is not a hindrance, but an asset which will increase children's linguistic awareness, cultural sensitivity and cognitive functioning'. Code switching and interlingual lexicon may not be desirable processes for linguists who would like to see each language to maintain its purity, but they are appropriate to young children and adults for communication and for expressing new ideas and concepts. For this, they should be encouraged rather than dismissed as a limitation and weakness.

Investing in story reading

Child-initiated learning provides the context to access children's immediate experience, interests and attention. However, new experiences too have an important function in extending children's learning. Adults may introduce such experiences through stories and story reading. All children love stories and grow particularly fond of those that become familiar to them. They know that stories have a structure: they have a beginning, an order and sequence of events and an ending. Such familiarity helps them to anticipate and predict the story plot, and to give and gain meaning.

The introduction of wordless and picture books may be the best way into story telling or reading. Their illustrations help the reader to achieve meaning through an understanding of the story plot. At the initial stages, in order to help children to attain meaning making, picture books should be chosen to have a high level of within-book intertextuality and low intertextual reference to the British culture. Books with high intertextuality may gradually be introduced as the children become more competent bilinguals (Evans, 1998; Laycock, 1998). Parents may also be invited into early years settings to read carefully selected picture books from the children's own languages and cultures.

Depending on the degree of bilingual competency among children, early years practitioners may read the story, discuss it with the children and encourage them to retell it. The illustrations can be used as an aid for intertextual signposting for children to make meaning and retell the story (Parkes, 1998). In child-initiated story telling children will often engage in role play, gestures, dramatic facial and body expressions, pictures, rhyme, music, props. This multi-sensory approach to story telling and retelling helps children to make multiple associations between different stimuli (auditory, visual, kinaesthetic, emotional etc.) to gain personal meaning from experience encountered in both language and cultures. Bruner (1990) reiterates such an approach when he claims that 'Logos and praxis' [that is words and actions] are culturally inseparable.

Parental and community support and resources

Language does not develop in a vacuum, and that applies to bilingualism. To support bilingual learners it is important to know their experiences within their families and communities, in addition to what they are doing in the setting. Some parents may systematically teach their children the mother tongue. In many cases where this happens their approaches differ from the approaches to language experience and development which children encounter in their early years settings. In many communities it is becoming common to see the provision of mother tongue classes. Often these are taught by volunteers who are not trained teachers or early years practitioners. They operate as after school clubs, and often have a formal and didactic approach. The implications of this are that children may be exposed to a variety of different contexts for language learning.

Information about the totality of children's exposure to these is important in order to make better use of their experiences and support their bilingual development in the most effective way, both at home and in the early years setting (Papatheodorou, 2007).

In conclusion

Supporting and maintaining bilingualism and creating multilingual early years settings is not an easy task. It requires consistent and systematic planning for developing everyday learning practices which:

- start from, invest and extend children's prior experience
- utilise bilingual learners' linguistic and cultural potential by giving frequent opportunities for child-initiated learning
- demonstrate genuine interest and curiosity in and respect for each child's language and culture in their self-initiated play
- create bilingual and multilingual inventories and books
- make use of story reading, telling and retelling, linked with role play and other multi-sensory activities
- encourage children to develop their own self-initiated role play
- make learning experiences fun and enjoyable and encourage children to initiate their own activities
- utilise family and community resources

Settings which follow these broad guidelines, and which give due weight to the encouragement of creativity and autonomy through the opportunities offered by child-initiated activities will do much to help their bilingual children and will be a beacon in their communities.

Bibliography and references

Arnberg, L. (1987), *Raising Children Bilingually: The Preschool Year*. Philadelphia: Bilingual Matters.

Baker, C. (2000), *A Parents' and Teachers' Guide to Bilingualism* (2nd edn), Clevedon: Multilingual Matters.

Barratt-Pugh, C. (2000), 'Literacies – More Than One Language', in C. Barratt Pugh and M. Rohl (eds) *Literacy Learning in the Early Years*, Buckingham: Open University Press.

Bialystok, E. (1991), *Language Processing in Bilingual Children*. New York: Cambridge University Press.

Bialystok, E. and Ryan, E. B. (1985), 'Toward a Definition of Metalinguistic Skill', Merrill-Palmer Quarterly Vol.31, pp. 229–51.

Bredekamp, S. and Copple, C. (eds) (1997), *Developmentally Appropriate Practice in Early Childhood Programs* (Revised edition), Washington DC: NAEYC.

Browne, A. (1996), *Developing Language and Literacy 3–8*. London: Paul Chapman.

Bruner, J. (1990), *Acts of Meaning*. Cambridge, Massachusetts: Harvard University Press.

Cavallaro, F. (2005), 'Language Maintenance Revisited: An Australian Perspective', *Bilingual Research Journal* Vol.29, No.3, pp.561–82.

Cummins, J. (2000), *Language, Power, and Pedagogy. Bilingual Children in the Crossfire*, Clevedon England: Multilingual Matters.

Evans, J. (1998), Introduction, in J. Evans (ed.) *What's in the Picture? Responding to Illustrations in Picture Books*. London: Paul Chapman.

Fishman, J. (1996), 'What Do You Lose When You Lose Your Language?' in G. Cantoni (ed.) (1996), *Stabilizing Indigenous Languages*. Flagstaff: Center for Excellence in Education, Northern Arizona University http://www.ncela.gwu.edu/pubs/stabilize/iii-families/lose.htm

Graham, J. (1998), 'Turning the Visual into the Verbal: Children Reading Wordless Books', in J. Evans (ed.) *What's in the Picture? Responding to Illustrations in Picture Books*. London: Paul Chapman.

Gregory, E. (1996), *Making Sense of a New World. Learning to Read in a Second Language*. London: Paul Chapman.

Kerper Mora, J., Wink, J. and Wink, D. (2001), 'Duelling Models of Dual Language Instruction: A Critical Review of the Literature and Program Implementation Guide'. *Bilingual Research Journal*, Vol.25, No.4, pp. 417–42.

Laycock, L. (1998), 'A Way into a New Language and Culture', in J. Evans (ed.) *What's in the Picture? Responding to Illustrations in Picture Books*. London: Paul Chapman.

McWilliam, N. (1998), *What's in a Word? Vocabulary Development in Multilingual Classrooms*. Stoke on Trent: Trentham.

Papatheodorou, T., Kainourgiou, E. and Dimas, K. (2006), 'Intercultural Preschool Pedagogy: Preliminary Findings from a Three-Country Study.' Paper presented at the 16th EECERA Conference, Reykjavik, Iceland.

Papatheodorou, T. (2007), 'Supporting the Mother Tongue: Pedagogical Approaches.' *Early Child Development and Care*, Vol. 177, No. 6, pp. 751–65.

Parkes, B. (1998), 'Nursery Children Using Illustrations in Shared Readings and Rereadings', in J. Evans (ed.) *What's in the Picture? Responding to Illustrations in Picture Books*. London: Paul Chapman

Souto-Manning, M. (2006), 'A Critical Look at Bilingualism Discourse in Public Schools: Autoethnographic Reflections of a Vulnerable Observer.' *Bilingual Research Journal*, Vol.30, No.2, pp. 559–77.

Tassoni, P. (2006), 'Tuning in, in S. Featherstone' (ed.) *Getting ready for phonics*, Featherstone, Bloomsbury Publishing plc.

Tse, L. (2001). 'Why Don't They Learn English?' *Separating Fact from Fallacy in the U.S. Language Debate*. New York: Teacher's College Press.

Whitehead M. R. (1997), *Language and Literacy in the Early years* (2nd edition). London: Paul Chapman.

Van der Veer, R. and Valsiner, J. (1991), *Understanding Vygotsky. A quest for synthesis*. Oxford: Blackwell.

Vygotsky, L. S. (1986), *Thought and Language* (3rd edition). Cambridge, MA: The MIT Press.

Sally Featherstone: Practice makes perfect: how the growing brain makes sense of experiences

> *Childhood is a process, not a product, and so is learning. In a society that respects products more than the processes of creation and thought, it is easy to fall into the trap of anxiety over measuring achievements in isolated skills. Have faith – in childhood and yourself. Children's brains generally seek what they need, and nature has given you the instincts to help them get it.*
>
> Jane Healy, *Your Child's Growing Brain*

At birth a baby's brain contains an estimated hundred thousand million brain cells, some of which are already talking to each other. How can we help babies and children to make further connection between these brain cells, strengthening and 'hard wiring' their experiences into learning for life?

What is actually happening in the brain during child-initiated play in a stimulating environment and in the company of sensitive adult and peer co-players? During this sort of activity the neurons (brain cells) in children's brains are fired up by the things the child chooses to do, sending signals through a single axon, and receiving signals through the many receiving dendrites of each cell. When new experiences are encountered and new discoveries made, links are formed between the neurons; hundreds of millions of them, inter-connecting as they snake through the tissue of the brain.

As babies and children continue to make links between their brain cells, those links which are revisited will be strengthened. Those which are not are likely to wither away. Turning 'soft' new wiring into 'hard wired' permanent learning is a key feature of childhood, and can be helped or hindered by the environment and by contact with other people. If children are not able to practise new learning, revisiting skills and abilities, the links between the neurons fade, putting the learning at risk of disappearing. This process is called 'neural pruning'. It is a survival mechanism. The brain has a lot of information to deal with, and so it jetissons anything that its experience tells it that it doesn't need. So if a new piece of information, a new experience, idea or skill is not confirmed by repeated visits the brain will dump it. It is the truth behind the expression 'use it or lose it'.

Children need to practise their newly acquired skills and interests in free play, or they are in danger of losing a lot of the skills we carefully teach them in adult-led or adult-directed activities. If you don't practise the song, you will forget the words; if you don't practise cutting you lose the muscular control and then the will to cut out; if you can't practise making a card after making one yesterday, you may lose the reason, purpose and thinking behind making the card.

> *Children need to rehearse in order to learn new skills. Without practice, new skills are lost. If you don't use it, you lose it; this is as true for cognitive skills as it is for muscles.*
> Ronald Kotulak, *Inside the Brain*

As children revisit and practise skills and language they return along previous neural pathways, and the revisiting has consequences. It's like making a footpath. Every journey along it makes the path more marked. Similarly, every trip back along a neural pathway strengthens and speeds up the link that the pathway provides. There's an important side effect too. Not only does the link itself get stronger, but also a protective coating is laid down on the link to preserve it and make it more permanent – 'hard wiring' it. This coating is a fatty substance called myelin, and it is produced by the body between birth and around 25, with one of its peaks in production between the ages of two and seven. Now we know why so much practice is so important in the early years. Not only are children making more links between brain cells than at any other time in their lives, but they are practising them and testing them as well, hard wiring and laying down myelin sheaths to preserve the connections they have confirmed.

> *Repeated use (of neural links) coats the axon (the cell transmitter) in a protective sheath called myelin. This process of myelination makes the transfer of information more efficient so that less neural space is needed.*
> Alistair Smith, *The Brain's Behind It*

Myelin is wonderful stuff, and we should be nurturing the conditions that favour its production. However there is a frightening feature of myelin: that is, its sensitivity to erosion by stress. Stress creates chemical reactions in the brain which actually destroy the myelin which coats the neural pathways. This erosion leaves the core connections open to damage, just as damaged insulation on a cable leaves an electrical connection vulnerable and at risk.

We should be aware of the effects of stress, from the unreasonable expectations of adults and organisations as well as from the pressures on children from life in modern society and the ambitions of aspiring, but sometimes ill-informed, parents.

Successful provision of opportunities for practice seems to have some key features. Being able to see the full range of equipment and resources available appears to be important, as brain research indicates that children may not be able to ask for, or even be conscious of, the particular resources or equipment their brain needs to practise and engage with. However, once they encounter them they know they need them. Haven't we all seen and remarked on the way a young child will seize upon a new resource? The child couldn't have told you that that was what it wanted, but it's clear that that is what its brain needed.

You may have seen children standing in the middle of your setting, turning round and round like a lighthouse until they suddenly see the person, place or equipment that will switch on their brain cells today. For some children, the lighthouse may be searching for an activity they were engaged in yesterday; for others, it is the 'scaffolded', more challenging version of yesterday's project, provided after observation by a conscientious practitioner; yet others may be searching for something new – a next step in learning, a new way of applying recently acquired skills, or a previously absorbing activity where new learning can be applied.

Michael Gurian described such activity in this way:

> For the developing brain, self-direction has many advantages, especially that in a supportive, well-led environment the mind gravitates towards learning what it needs to learn in order to grow. The brain has, to a great extent, its own blueprint of how to grow itself, and if a classroom is set up to let the brain explore, it moves in the neural motions required.
>
> Michael Gurian, *Boys and Girls Learn Differently*

If children need to ask or search behind cupboard doors for the resources they need they may just wander, trying activity after activity in the search for the learning trigger that will switch on their attention and concentration. Practitioners should be aware of this need when organising and setting up their indoor and outdoor environments, making sure that visibility, not just accessibility, is a key feature.

The answer is not to choose activities for the children, putting these out in an engaging way on tables and carpets. Limiting the choice to the activities we think children need to experience in fact often does just the opposite from what we intend. It reduces their choices, the space for their own play, and their ability to select from the full range of opportunities. We should no longer try to be the elves in 'The Elves and the Shoemaker', tiptoeing around when the children are in bed, selecting and displaying a few carefully and artistically arranged resources for them to choose from when they wake. Instead, we should be concentrating on making our settings exciting, well organised, well labelled and signposted so children know where things are and can select from them, sure that there will be plenty of space to explore their chosen activity and that there will be interested support from adults.

Of course this knowledge about children's brains and learning is not without pressures, particularly in settings where space is limited. Children need to continue to see and access resources that they may seem to have mentally, physically or developmentally outgrown, as well as those currently in use. This is important because they need to be able to revisit earlier experiences, applying new abilities and thinking to previous understanding. Retrieving an old favourite toy from the dustbin or rummage sale, or loving a chance to return to a previous class, now makes sense. It's not just sentimentality or the comfort of security (although it may contain both these feelings); it's a real learning need, a chance to demonstrate new skills in an old activity or with objects previously outgrown!

The ideal 'brain-growing environment' may seem to indicate that the variety and range of equipment needed for each age group should be endless. However, another feature of children's brains is that they are more likely to be switched on by open-ended and flexible resources than by closed ones that require little or no creativity or invention on their part, nor those with a target age range printed on the box. Examples of closed resources are toys and games that have few or a limited number of functions or uses. Examples of open-ended resources are things you can use in lots of different ways: drainpipes, rope, string, boxes, fabric lengths, clothes pegs, buckets, bags, planks, tyres, crates, recycled materials. These things are far more stimulating and engaging than those which have only one purpose.

In an open-ended, freely chosen environment, the role of the practitioner is to watch, listen and ask open questions. She will model techniques and language, responding to children's needs and interests, and trying not to interfere or imply that she knows best. This is not easy, but it does underpin the international evidence that observation of children in free, child-initiated learning will tell us more about what they know and can do than any test or adult-directed task.

Trying to speed learning over unfinished neuron systems might be akin to racing a limousine over a narrow path in the woods. You can do it, but neither the car nor the path ends up in very good shape! Moreover, the pressure that surrounds such learning situations may leave permanent emotional debris.

Jane Healy, *Your Child's Growing Brain*

Even in a freely chosen programme, there are things that adults can do to engage children's interests by 'tempting them in'. Experienced practitioners know that there are lots of ways you can fascinate children into practicing and extending learning or skills (as long as you are prepared for your suggestions to be ignored or swept aside!). You can try,

- leaving opportunities to repeat a small group of activities from the day before, to engage those children whose brains need more practice (materials to make more cards or letters, a phonic basket of toys, a story bag and tape)
- adding some fresh materials to a current area of interest (some ribbons on the craft table, a building magazine in the builders' role play, a new story and puppet in the book area)
- providing a new, flexible resource for the play (a piece of unwanted carpet in your outside area, a box from a washing machine, a collection of fallen leaves you picked up on a Sunday walk, goggles and a snorkel tube)
- responding to requests from children (Can we have somewhere to wash the dolls' clothes? Have you got another tea-set? We want to have a picnic. We need some big elastic bands and a post box.)

Your responsiveness may be just the stimulus that the children need to take an interest further, extending their neural pathways and confirming those already formed.

The time allocation and timing of child-initiated learning during the day and the week should also be informed by the conclusions of research into brain development. The provision of this period of play in HighScope settings and other locations where similar philosophies have been adopted, has traditionally been at the beginning of the session – preferably right at the start when, following self-registration, children discuss and plan what they will do, with all the resources (including all the adults) available to them. The effectiveness of this commitment, founded in the research available in the 1960s, has now been confirmed. For both the emotional and the cognitive development of young children, the ideal time for the provision of ree-flow indoor/outdoor play is at the beginning of part-time or full-time provision. There are good reasons for this.

Starting the day with formal, adult-directed activity is discouraging to children's natural intentions, because they can see things their brains need to engage with but they are not permitted to engage with them. They are told to sit down, keep still, work on the activity they've been given. Meanwhile their minds are tugging at these adult imposed leashes, longing to be free and to get at what they really want – really need – to do. This is frustrating, and we know that stress and frustration will erode current and previous learning by releasing chemicals in the brain which destroy the protective myelin coating on the neural pathways.

Encouraging brain cells to make links with each other is the key professional activity for everyone working with children between birth and five – parents, carers, practitioners and their managers. It is now clear that recent research into brain development in the early years has influenced governments in many countries and on all continents, and where this has happened it has resulted in a focus on high quality provision in the early years. This is not least in response to the long-term benefits in reducing crime and social exclusion, and increasing stability in those adults who have experienced such high quality early education. The resulting financial investment, although not always well targeted or managed, acknowledges the need to build the best possible brains before the age of five.

> The quality of the environment and the kind of experiences children have may affect brain structure and functioning so profoundly that they may not be correctable after the age of five.
>
> Ronald Kotulak, *Inside the Brain*

Headstart, HighScope, SureStart, Te Whariki, Reggio Emilia, and many of the other early childhood settings and approaches which are generally regarded as being in the forefront of good practice, share a common view. All of them focus closely on the importance of child-initiated learning in a well resourced and stimulating environment, in the company of interested adults. This is in harmony with and supports the latest thinking on brain development.

Experienced practitioners also tell us that time is a critical feature in maintaining lasting learning during child-initiated periods, and this is supported by research in settings. Sessions that last too long, particularly with little adult support, can turn into unproductive and often destructive play, where probably the only things that children are learning is that their play (the most important activity in their eyes) is of little interest to the adults. Where there is plenty of support and the environment is carefully organised and well resourced, children will remain engaged for substantial periods of time. Of course, the quality as well as the quantity of support is a key feature. Where adults model and use relevant language and good questioning techniques, children's thinking and language development is enhanced and their play is enriched. Daily periods of child-initiated play of between three quarters of an hour and an hour and a half are not uncommon in effective settings and schools.

> *Brain research asks that at least a third of the day be reserved for self direction. A successful teacher in the early years often finds that some children can support more than half a day of self direction.*
> Michael Gurian, (2001) *Boys and Girls learn Differently*

Supporting skills development is an important part of the process. Simply waiting until the child becomes interested in acquiring a new skill, or dealing with the request of one child at a time, are not effective uses of practitioner time. Responding to observations of children pursuing self-chosen activities will reveal the level of their skills in all areas of learning, and will give practitioners key information about when or whether to involve individual children in extending their gross or fine motor, language or listening abilities and skills, or the development of their mathematical or creative thinking. This information can be used to identify individuals and groups of children who would benefit from more targeted activities in small or larger groups.

> *Since the child's frameworks are small and immature, her learning in any situation is qualitatively different from yours. You can try to lend her your schemas (hooks for learning) by explaining them, but if she lacks the personal experience, your words will fall right off her incomplete hooks. This may explain why each generation seems to have to make its own mistakes instead of taking the advice of its elders!*
> Jane Healy, *Your Child's Growing Brain*

Adult-directed, and even adult-led or adult-initiated tasks and activities will only be effective in reinforcing learning if they are relevant to the child, building on previous experiences in a meaningful and engaging way. This is the art of good practice, ensuring a seamless join between children's current interests and stage of development and opportunities to move into Vygotsky's 'zone of proximal development'

– the difference between what a learner can do without help and what she or he can do with help.

So what are the key messages for practitioners from recent research into young brains?

- Practice is vital in converting soft wiring into hard wiring
- Myelin protects neural links as they become hard wired, and is damaged by stress
- Practice should involve children in activities which follow their interests and are freely chosen
- Settings and classrooms should be set up to enable free, unfettered visual and physical access to resources
- Selecting activities for the children is likely to result in stress rather than development
- Observing children as they play will give practitioners information on which they should base future plans and activities
- Children need to learn new skills which build on their existing abilities and interests
- The timing and support for, and the value of child-initiated learning is just as important as the activity itself

Anne Meade, an early childhood specialist in New Zealand, undertook some research in 1995 into the development of schemas, the repetitive behaviours children display during their play. She had this to say about the child-centred curriculum, where play is initiated by the children themselves. It inspired the title of this book, as it so clearly describes the behaviour of young children as they turn their previous learning into a permanent understanding:

> When observing young children in an early childhood centre that is using a child-centred curriculum, adults often think they are like butterflies, flitting from area to area, from child to child. That may be true some of the time. However, when integrated learning is taking place, another metaphor might be more appropriate; that of bees which gather nectar to integrate into something of significance. Children focus their attention by fitting new experiences into patterns they have already stored in their memories. They develop schemas by behaving like honey bees, moving from experience to experience to gather further ingredients to encode; in that way they build a

fuller understanding of that schema. In other words, children get hooked on certain patterns of behaviour because they are trying to make sense of the abstract characteristics of particular features of their environment.

Anne Meade, *Thinking Children*

As we embark on the implementation of yet another version of the national framework for learning in the early years, a subject of continuing interest to practitioners across the world, we need to focus on HOW children learn, not just on WHAT they learn. The newly re-structured Characteristics of Effective Learning (www.foundationyears.org.uk) makes a good starting place for us all:

Playing and exploring – engagement
- Finding out and exploring
- Playing with what they know
- Being willing to 'have a go'

Active learning – motivation
- Being involved and concentrating
- Keeping trying
- Enjoying achieving what they set out to do

Creating and thinking critically – thinking
- Having their own ideas
- Making links
- Choosing ways to do things

Bibliography and references

Department for Education (2012), *Statutory Framework for the Early Years Foundation Stage*.

Early Education, for the DFE (2012), *Development Matters in the Early Years Foundation Stage*, www.foundationyears.org.uk

Gurian, Michael. (2001), *Boys and Girls Learn Differently*. Hoboken, NJ: Jossey Bass.

Healy, Jane. (2004), *Your Child's Growing Brain*. New York: Broadway Books.

Kotulak, Ronald. (1997), *Inside the Brain*. Riverside, NJ: Andrews McMeel.

Meade, Anne. (1995), *Thinking Children*. Wellington: New Zealand Council for Educational Research.

Smith, Alistair. (2004), *The Brain's Behind It*. London: Network Continuum.